THE FUTURE OF MAN
BY EDWARD C. RANDALL

ORIGINALLY PUBLISHED IN 1908

The Future of Man by Edward C. Randall
This book edition was created and published by Mamba Press
©MambaPress 2024. All Rights Reserved.

Contents

Foreword
    I. The Great Question
    II. The Mental Grasp
    III. Truth And Appearance
    IV. Progress
    V. How Do I Know?
    VI. Spirit Identity
    VII. Of Many Minds
    VIII. Speech With Spirit-People
    IX. Thought And Mind
    X. Nature's Laboratory
    XI. Vibration
    XII. Matter
    XIII. Limitations Of Science
    XIV. The Attitude Of Science
    XV. Evolution
    XVI. Beyond The Atom
    XVII. The Subconscious Mind
    XVIII. Spirit-Suggestion
    XIX. The World's Desire
    XX. Homes In The After Life
    XXI. True Charity
    XXII. "To That Mortal Would I Speak."
    XXIII. Truth At Last

Foreword

IN the presence of dissolution of faith, belief and creeds wither and decay, and doubt goes hand in hand with grief. In such a presence we feel what speech cannot tell, and hope that what seems night here is somewhere else a dawn. In the majesty of this silence, how acts and deeds bust into perfect form. When loving hearts are breaking, and heads are bowed above an open grave, how dare any priest presume to tell what he does not know?

Little at best can be known of the afterlife, so boundless is its scope; yet enough can be learned while in the body, to dispel the awful fear and to lighten the sorrows that fill the human heart, as well as to make men lead better lives because they can live more intelligently, and so enrich the world. That I may increase this knowledge, I have investigated every natural law that I have had the opportunity and ability to study, and now, owing to present freedom of speech, I publish the results of my investigation without fear. In many ways I have sought the thought of men, both in and out of the body, ever drawing my own conclusions, and making my own deductions, I have felt the thrill of success in the discovery of new laws and in the proving of new facts.

The bridge of death no longer rests upon the clouds of hope, but upon great piers of knowledge. Every act is but the product of conditions, and the heart applauds the brain when one works to increase the force of universal good. I know that matter is eternal and that only form is new, and that one who but yesterday in the flush of health faced the storms of life with splendid courage, and whose body lies to-night in the embrace of mother earth, is no exception to the rule. All that was matter, as we use the term, the outer garment, all that gave him physical expression, will mingle with the substance from which it was formed: but his spirit is eternal, his progression will be unbroken, and his horizon will widen, as he reaches the sphere of psychic discovery. I know that to the limits of that plane in which he lives at first, the human voice will carry, the thought will reach. The so-called dead live here about us, know our sorrows and grieve with us. They share our happiness, they know our hopes and ambitions, and, by suggestion, through our sub-conscious brain, they influence our daily conduct. I know that there in the after-life they have feature, form and expression, and, therefore, bodies composed of matter, for there cannot be form without substance. The substance that forms the bodies of spirit-people, vibrating more than five octaves higher than the violet ray, few in earth-life ever see, though spirit people see and talk with each other, and with mortals when the necessary conditions are secured. I know that every hope, ambition and desire of earth are continued beyond this life, as is also the burden of wrong. I know that we are as much spirit now as we ever shall be; that in death, so-called, we simply vacate and discard the gross material that gives us expression in this physical plane. All about this material world of ours, there exists, in fact, the psychic or spiritual universe, more active and real than this, peopled with all the countless dead, who, no longer burdened with a physical body, move at will within the boundaries of their sphere, in what appears as space to mortal man.

Their life is an active one. All the new conditions, all the great laws by which they are to be governed, must be learned, and only by individual effort can they live intelligently and well. I know that a wrong act in earth-life must be lived over again in the next sphere, and lived right, before advancement is possible; that the labor is often long, but that families and friends are, in time, reunited and take up the thread where it was broken. I have heard them talk among themselves, and to me, and many eminent men and women, upon my invitation, have heard the same that I have heard in the material conditions that we have made. I know something of the democracy of death, and that all mankind is beginning to hear and march to the silent music of reason. I know, too, that the highest duty of every one is to contribute what he can to the prosperity of the many, who though rich in worldly goods, are mentally poor in a land of opportunity, and that this individual life of ours, whether it has had birth within the palace or the hut, no matter how it turns and curves and falls among the hills as it courses from the mountain-tops, through valley-lands, or, lies at times in stagnant pools of ignorance and vice, festering in the sun, must some day reach the great ocean of eternal life, from whence it came, clean and pure.

I am told that: "Beyond the life men call material, is another so much more real, so much more vital and interesting, that, when you enter into its fullest harmony, the little lives you led on earth will fade into the dim unreality of a dream-like past.

We cannot in the nature of things know much of the every-day life of spirits who people what to us is infinite space, because we are unable to grasp, to any great extent, the realities of their conditions. All can learn a little of matter and laws that control it beyond the physical plane, and to that extent can reason from cause to effect, without which there cannot be any rational conclusion.

I know that the tendency of all people is to do right, and that an invisible world, peopled by the so-called dead of all ages past, is interested in and is aiding our progression, that it speaks to our dull ears, with silent voices heard only through the subconscious brain; and I know that the great desire and hope of those beyond is to bring the world to an understanding of what dissolution means and of what follows so-called death, so that, knowing these two things, they may learn how to live the earthlife well.

The age of faith is past. The teaching of the church no longer satisfies the hunger of heart and brain. This is an age of fact. The present calls upon all men to think, not to believe; the torch of reason has been lighted, and its day is here. Some of the churches are now teaching mental therapeutics and utilizing psychic force to heal the sick, and, in time, all must follow the example of the few. The education and development of this generation have made it possible for spirit-intelligence to direct, in some measure, the thought and conduct of mankind; and so I thoroughly believe the churches that shall teach the truth are already built.

For many years, I have been associated with two distinguished gentlemen and, with the aid of a psychic, talked *voice* to *voice* with spirit-people. Possessing no unusual ability or powers, we have been obliged to develop one who possesses psychic force. Having observed the conditions required by spirit-people, we have found another and a busy active world here and about us, in which people live and move in such intense vibration, that they are not visible to the physical eye. They inhabit what we know as space and have, under certain conditions, power to speak to mortal man. Many of the so-called dead have honored us with their friendship and have given us much instruction. When I have used their own words, the fact is indicated by quotation marks.

I have written these pages with the hope that some heart, heavy with sorrow, may come to comprehend the truth about dissolution, and to know that those called dead are alive, and that all is well with them. We should ever look with eager eyes for gems of truth, and what we find, we should have the courage to express. I know better than anyone can tell me, how incomplete is this effort to give the world a Metapsychic Philosophy, but bear with me: I have gone, in my research, beyond physical laws and the books of men, out into the wilderness of fact; beyond the beaten path into another world, more active and more real than the one in which we live, and what I have written, incomplete though it may be, *are facts* and *they are true.* Without arrogance, prejudice or preconceived and fixed notions, I have sat at the feet of learning, and, with eager and receptive brain, have listened to the teachings of splendid minds beyond the physical sphere and have weighed carefully each word in the light of reason and of experience. I know "there is no death; there are no dead;" that this life is but the creative plane, a preparatory stage of development for the reality that comes with dissolution, which is merely an increasing of our vibratory action. This is the greatest discovery of the present age, and, when appreciated, will revolutionize the thought and conduct of the generation that shall accept it.

Some mortal lives are so lived that they stand out like trees aflame along the green and wooded shore where waters beat with endless wave; others, like undergrowth within the endless forest, remain unknown, but each must, according to the immutable laws of progression, at some time, obtain perfect development, which is the heritage of all: this is the law of life.

I know that in the kingdom of the mind there can be no personal dictation; that there is no God but universal good; no Savior but one's self; no trinity but matter, force and mind.

The twilight of fear has become to us, who know this phase of life, a sacred hour, when, as the shadows fall, and rest follows a day of labor, we call to those beyond and hear voices of those so-called dead tell us of the future life of man.

Dated Buffalo, N. Y., Oct. 101 h, 1908.

Edward C. Randall.

In the beginning, one of my co-workers, in the life beyond, said:

"I find about you, Mr. Randall, a crowd of earnest spirit-people who are bending all their thought upon this which you are about to undertake. They will help you, when writing, by their suggestions, and, as the little book begins its journey to find the hearts of men, they will open many doors, and guide it to many darkened homes. The light illuminating every page will be the beacon for many in distress, and we in spirit do most sincerely thank you for your efforts to bring these great truths to all people.

"We see so many entering spirit-life who have lived and died ignorant of this natural law, and we know so well the importance of knowing and living according to that law, that we rejoice over this book of knowledge and we will speed it on its helpful journey with eagerness and with pleasure."

I. The Great Question

SINCE mankind came up out of savagery, the great problem has been and ever shall be: What is the ultimate end of man? What, if anything, waits on the other side of death's mysterious door? What happens when the hour strikes that closes man's career, when, leaving all the gathered wealth of lands and goods, he goes out into the dark alone? Is death the end—annihilation and repose? Or, does he wake in some other sphere or condition, retaining individuality and identity?

Each must solve this great question, whether he like it or not. Dissolution and change have come to every form of life, and will come to all that live. With opportunity knocking at the door, mankind has but little more appreciation of it now than it had when Phallic-worship swayed the destinies of empires. It may be that, as a people, our development has been such that we could heretofore grasp and comprehend only length, breadth and thickness, the three accepted dimensions of matter; that in our progression we have *but now* become able to appreciate and understand life forces that find their only expression beyond the physical plane.

This was when all knowledge was handed down from one generation to another by story, song and tradition. When the Persian civilization was growing old and ambition towered above the lofty walls of Babylon; when Egypt was building her temples on the banks of the Nile; when Greece was the center of art and culture, and Rome with its wealth and luxuries held sway over the civilized world, they did not dream of type and printing press or applied electricity, and the many inventions in connection therewith that were yet to come. Those people were not ready for such progression.

The world cannot stand still. The great law of the universe is progress. Two or three generations since, the idea that a cable would one day be laid under the sea and that messages would be transmitted under the waters from continent to continent, was laughed at as a chimera. Only a little while ago, the world could not understand how words and sentences could be flashed across the trackless ocean from ship to ship, and from land to land, without wires, in space. And who shall now say that it is not possible to send thoughts, words, sentences, voices even, and messages, out into the ether of the spirit world, there to be heard, recorded and answered? Has man reached the end of his possibilities; will all progression stop with Marconi's achievements?

This is the age of man; we have passed the age of the gods. If our development is such that we can comprehend the life and the conditions following dissolution, it must be within our grasp as surely as progress has been possible at all times and among all people since the world began.

Great changes are at hand. There are to-day, political, financial and religious revolutions. Honest men are demanded for public office; the day of the corruptionist is passing. Captains of finance, who manipulate trust funds for personal gain in violation of law, fear imprisonment. Priests are realizing that they are no longer regarded as infallible; congregations have ceased to accept their conclusions or interpretations of one great natural law; the pulpit is losing attraction, and church attendance is slowly, but surely, diminishing. People are doing their own thinking, and with thought comes doubt, the dawn of reason, the stepping stone to the temple of knowledge.

Assuming, then, that we have come to that period, when we can look upon all subjects and propositions impartially and intelligently, no longer bound by fear, past or present, and can open the book of life, we now appreciate that it is of the greatest importance to know what follows this life.

We are swinging away from the old moorings; new views come with changing times and conditions. Knowledge is the torch that fires our enthusiasm and makes advancement possible. It is not the past but the future that commands our attention. We may learn much of nature as she speaks, in all dialects, her various tongues.

All truth is safe, nothing else will suffice, and he who holds back the truth, through expediency or fear, fails in his duty to mankind.

Our age is one of sudden and rapid changes; the people are in a state of transition. Most minds are sensitive and each must be alert and versatile. It is a period fraught with unrest and thirst for knowledge. What was true yesterday, assumes a different, one could almost say a diametrically opposite aspect, to-day. This is a period that will be fruitful in great wonders in scientific discoveries, and in the adaptation of the universal law of vibratory action. Much that is said now could not have been explained a year ago.

Some have come to know what awaits over the great divide, have solved the great problem of dissolution, and with the confidence born of knowledge, based on facts proved and demonstrated, are ready to speak with authority. As one among the many, I again give the world the result of my continued research in the new science of Metapsychics.

The thought that there need be no more groping in the dark, makes the pulse quicken. The realization that fear can now be eliminated from the human brain, fills every heart with joy. The fact that we may come into touch with those in spheres beyond and know that they live, and how and where they live, will lift the burden of sorrow from every heart that mourns its dead.

The child learns readily for two reasons, viz: (a) It has no preconceived notions or fixed ideas; (b) it has nothing to unlearn: its mind is free and receptive. We, of older growth, are but children in the wilderness of these new and subtle laws. Before we can grasp and comprehend this philosophy, we must free our minds and eliminate false conceptions and erroneous ideas. That this is a difficult task I well know, for minds filled with traditions and false conceptions of the after-life, simply cannot comprehend the truth when it is given to them. There can be no individual progression until one becomes free, mentally poised, open to reason and willing to hear facts and to weigh them honestly. The blind are entitled to our sympathy; we look upon those who cannot grasp a truth, because it is not as they have been taught, with sorrow; but we grasp the open hands of the free and walk with them in nature's highway and reason with them.

Humanity is awakening. For two thousand years it has listened to the song and drone of priest and preacher, and, lulled into a sense of security, has lived indifferent to the end which each one fast approaches. The mind has, at last, become active, and now demands to know what fate awaits us beyond the grave. Man has learned something about himself and the universe, and this knowledge has made him free. He is no longer in spiritual bondage. This is an age of intellectual emancipation. Those who walk with open eyes will find the truth, for it lights the way across the continent of every human life.

II. The Mental Grasp

MANY will read the facts that are stated in this work and utterly fail to comprehend them or to grasp the laws that make such conditions possible. This I know from my own experience, for it took many years of research, study and deductive reasoning for me to comprehend, in a limited way, life in the physical apart from gross matter. The trouble was in the imperfect mental grasp.

When Copernicus said that the earth moved around the sun, and not the sun around the earth, as had been held since the end of Egyptian astronomy, the voice of all Europe was raised in protest against such a proposition; people could not comprehend such a fact, for it appeared to them that, if the earth moved from one side of a vast orbit to the other, the stars would be displaced. Tycho Brahe, the great mathematician, gave up the Copernican theory because he said, if true, his brain could not comprehend the magnitude of the universe. Bruno was put to death for defending the proposition, and it took a century for this truth to be realized, so contrary was it to the former teaching and belief.

After Cassini upset the observations of Hooke and Flamstead, Molyneaux, an amateur, constructed the "zenithsector," and measured the distances of stars, but many years elapsed before this fact was accepted, for the human brain could not realize such tremendous distances. And Roemer, when he measured the speed of light, met the same reception and died before his discovery was accepted. The age could not grasp the stupendous conception; such inconceivable velocities were too terrific, and the minds of able men were overwhelmed and confounded in the majestic and awful presence of nature.

We are told that on a clear night, 6874 stars, from the brightest to the sixth magnitude, are visible without optical aid, half of them being above the horizon at the same time. Down to the present time, more than one million others have, with the aid of the telescope, been counted with more or less accuracy. Sirius, the brightest of all, is seven hundred thousand times farther from our earth than the sun, and it would take ten thousand stars of the eleventh magnitude and one million of the sixteenth, to emit the quantity of light poured forth by the mighty Aldebaran. Every star is really a colossal sun at terrific heat, and the center of a solar system like our own. Who shall say how many more shall be found in the depth of infinite space? To the average mind these facts and figures mean nothing; such distances are incomprehensible; such numbers stagger us; we have heretofore had nothing with which to compare them. No *mortal* has journeyed to other planets or suns, or gone such distances; therefore, these facts are practically beyond the mental grasp, like many here presented. Any subject outside one's knowledge and experience is beyond his comprehension.

It is a law that knowledge, which precedes appreciation, must be acquired by individual effort, by study, by labor, deduction, reason; and, as the world has devoted its research almost entirely to matter, meaning thereby matter in its lowest form, it is, therefore, densely ignorant of anything beyond the physical plane.

When anyone fails to understand the simple facts here presented, it is because he has not carried his observation beyond the physical, for I have discovered only what anyone can by making well-directed and persistent effort. The situation as to these propositions is not very different now from what it was when Copernicus discovered the earth's movement, except that they do not now burn men for proclaiming a new discovery. It is as difficult for the mass of people to realize today that there is an invisible world about us, filled with actual people, as it was when Bruno lived, to comprehend the movements of this earth.

When I say that there is life after so-called death, and that spirit people have form, feature, individuality, identity and occupation; that this world invisible to our physical eye is here, on and about this earth, and in what we know as space; when I say that those thought to be dead walk our streets, enter our homes, and are with us much as before, the great majority can no more comprehend such a condition of things than they can the number of stars in the sky or the distance of Sirius, the brightest of our constellations, or what the parallax of Canopus is. I know of the after-life by reason of having talked with thousands of persons now there, who have proved identity in a most emphatic manner; but, after many years of conversation with spirit-people, I frankly admit that I can comprehend only in a limited way their life and environment, so different is it from the physical. If I do fail to comprehend their daily life fully, what will one do who has never devoted an hour to the study of matter and life-forces in their higher vibratory conditions?

We should not expect to understand and appreciate individual progression beyond the physical, or where and how people live in the next sphere, from an abstract statement of the fact. To gain knowledge of this condition, we must approach this vast problem as we would any other great subject we desire to master. First, we must know something of the origin of physical life, how it is started, how it develops and grows; the object of material existence; how soul and body are nourished and held together; something of the theory of heartaction, blood circulation and the vibratory conditions of matter; what dissolution really means; what life-force is and where it comes from; the effect of conduct here on conditions in the after-life, and how to live so as to enrich ourselves when we cast aside that physical substance that gives us expression. These propositions, stupendous as they seem, are in fact only elementary, and their mastery is a condition precedent to appreciation of life and environment in spirit-spheres. Knowledge on this subject, as in any other field of research, must be acquired by study. You would not expect to know the history of the earth's evolution and movements without studying geology and gravity, or the difference in the flora without knowing something of botany, or the chemical constituents of matter without the study of chemistry. The same law applies to psychic force and to life beyond the earth-plane, as on the earth-plane. It is a great science—a wholly new philosophy. Few intelligent minds have ever entered this great field of knowledge; little effort has been systematically expended on it, and the results are, at best, only commensurate with the effort. No one man, or class of men, can bring these laws comprehensively to the human mind. All who study the subject can help, but the knowledge and appreciation that will reach the inner chamber of thought must be acquired by individual effort born of the desire to know. Those who cannot comprehend new propositions, must remember there are problems in trigonometry that many do not understand; but if we commence with simple mathematics, and work along step by step, they will become as simple to us as the multiplication table. The same process must be used if we would grasp the principles and laws of Metapsychics. Abstract statements are of little value except to stimulate interest. Effort and well-directed study are of great importance. There are no schools or universities where this philosophy is taught, and few are qualified to teach it. Few books have been written that one can accept. But, for all that, one has nature all about him, at all times, calling in all tongues, and in all languages. The fact that life is everywhere, that nothing can die or be destroyed, speaks to our dull senses in a thousand ways; sings of joy and peace through the forest-trees and woos us with bud, flower and growing grain. But so blind is the world that but few can read intelligently the book of nature, ever open to view. It is the great misfortune of the human race that these laws, more important than others that have been mastered, are practically unknown, though the peace and happiness of everyone depend upon an understanding of them.

Let me make a more simple statement. Before all form is mind. The desk I write on, the pen I use, the chair upon which I sit, the books on the shelves, the rugs on the floor, the lamp on the table, and the telephone on the wall, every machine that moves; each was conceived and fashioned in the mind before it was physically constructed. All matter, as we use that term, is the expression of thought; every planet in our solar system and all the countless suns that light the night, are but the expressions of thought.

All the great discoveries of modern times are simple when understood; the difficulty is with the understanding. When once we know the why and the wherefore, all natural laws become so plain that "he who runs may read." What we cannot grasp, we regard as mysterious. When we discover one of nature's laws, we marvel at its simplicity. There is nothing in nature that is supernatural; there is no supernormal, these are but names given to conditions not understood.

The working and development of a human mind is intensely interesting. Mr. K., who spent one year with me in this research, was a man of much learning and a great thinker along material lines, and when I endeavored to explain life, apart from the physical, it was so different from his experience that he was at first utterly unable to grasp it. As we progressed, step by step, confining our discussion to cause and effect, he came to appreciate the force of simple facts, and when he heard and talked, voice to voice, with spirit-people, his progress was wonderful, he could appreciate the fact and the reason for it. On the other hand, I tried for weeks, with as simple words as I could use, to explain this philosophy to another who was anxious to know, but who had an untrained mind, practically without making any impression. The one was a thinker and a worker; the other was indolent and undeveloped mentally, and consequently had a limited grasp of such facts.

From these experiences, and many others, I conclude that the vast majority of mankind, having but little knowledge of this subject, cannot appreciate much beyond the visible and tangible, though they may be learned in other ways. Individual life, beyond the physical and similar to it, will be hard for many to grasp, because they have not investigated the elementary laws that form the groundwork of Metapsychics.

If I can arouse human beings from their indifference to this great question, more vital to them than money, and get them interested in this new philosophy, they will find the truth in their own way. For a thousand years the individual has lived in fear, bound by creeds and dogmas, and has been told what he should and should not do, how he must think, what he must think,—a slave to superstition and prejudice. But fear no longer sways the mind, superstitions have been outgrown, creeds have lost their meaning, and prejudice, the child of ignorance, no longer dominates the way on the crowded avenue of knowledge.

III. Truth And Appearance

TRUTH is always an achievement; it becomes such by reversing appearances, turning rest into motion, solids into fluids, centers into orbits, and by breaking up inclosing firmaments into infinite space. The sun, the moon, the stars seem to revolve, but they do not. We feel that the earth is motionless; that idea is erroneous too. We see the sun rise above the horizon; it is beneath us. We touch what we think is a solid body; there is no such thing. We think we hear harmonious sounds; but the air has only brought us silent undulations. We admire the effects of light, and the colors that bring vividly before our eyes the splendid scenes of nature; but in fact there is no light, there are no colors. It is the movement of colorless ether striking on our optic nerve which gives us the impression of light and color. We speak of heat and cold; there is neither heat nor cold in the universe, only motion.

Once it was said "This is as it appears." Now we say "The reality is not according to first appearance, but usually the reverse." Knowledge has reversed these beliefs, and the contrary is now proved to be the fact. The energy of an active agent seems to end with disorganization, but it really passes into another form. The appearance of nature is almost always elusive; and our first interpretation of natural conditions is usually the reverse of the reality. Of course this must be so; *it is the wisdom of creation and the secret of the world; else knowledge would be immediate and without process.* Nature has put reality at a distance, and a natural law compels each to travel that distance, and, by labor and study, to distinguish reality from appearance.

Dissolution is no exception to the universal law. It is not as it appears, but the contrary. Death is only another birth into a more active condition. Those whom we call dead simply move into a new community, leaving mankind, because of their unenlightened condition, appalled at the change. There is nothing in the great scheme of nature that, when understood, is not simple, harmonious and beautiful. Many look at dissolution with horror because they do not understand what it is and to what it leads. Fear is the lowest of human emotions, and the child of ignorance. When we all come to such a stage of mental progress that we can understand, we shall appreciate the wisdom and necessity of dissolution. Were it not for death, as we call it, this world would be crowded to starvation. Were it not for pain, we should not be warned against danger nor should we know how to avert it. Sickness is a necessity; and all punishment that results from violation of nature's laws, is disciplinary. Dissolution only shifts the scenes, and transfers the individual from a material to a spiritual stage of action, without taking from or adding to his moral or intellectual capacity. In the next sphere of action, he no longer sees with half a vision, but is brought face to face with himself, which gives a higher, broader and more comprehensive view and understanding of the economy of existence, which is evolution—a law as unalterable and indestructible as the mind itself.

If a man never becomes more than he is now, the whole process of evolution, by which he has come to be what he is, turns on itself. The benevolent purpose, seen at every stage as it yields to the next, stops its progression, dies out, and goes no further ; the little bubble of existence that has grown and distended till it reflects reality in all its glorious tints, bursts in a moment into nothingness. Life has been given to us forever; it is the only one of all the gifts that nature will never take from us. This body of ours may decay on some desert or plain, it may mould and go back to dust from which it came; but the life will never be extinguished. The breath is not the life of man; it only keeps in motion the wonderful mechanism that holds spirit in the physical plane. The soul, the spirit, the self, never dies.

Life beyond the grave is the promise that hope has ever whispered to all who have lived; but it has taken more ages than those of which we have a record for evolution to develop the mental faculties so that they can grasp these more advanced conditions where evidence is obtainable, and to demonstrate the fact. Time was when every cradle asked us whence, and every coffin asked whither, and this generation, for the first time in history, answers these questions intelligently. Unfortunately, the average individual has formed erroneous conceptions concerning the after-life, and these must be corrected before he can appreciate the sublime standard of natural law, and stand erect beside the column of knowledge, from which flares the inextinguishable torch of reason.

The sovereignty of the individual must be gained by effort in the manner nature has decreed. The mind is so constructed that truth and error cannot occupy the same place at the same time; and when one attempts to understand a new condition, the one must be ejected before the other can enter. It has ever required greater effort to get rid of the false than to acquire the true. The weak must be taught. The strongest at some time must bend and obey. Should anyone who reads this new philosophy fail to grasp these laws, let him ask himself the reason, and see whether there are not two causes: (a) preconceived notions based on what one has been told, of which there is no proof; and (b) unfamiliarity with the conditions and laws in force beyond the physical.

No man, however well he may have mastered the laws of the material universe, should consider himself qualified to pass judgment on the conditions following dissolution, until he knows something of matter in its higher vibratory conditions; for in this domain only is intense life found. These laws, like those pertaining wholly to gross matter, cannot be comprehended until the mind is free and open to conviction, and has evidence from which deductions may be drawn. The eternal dome of thought is high and broad, and each should do what he can to change the night of intellectual darkness into perfect day. Every man who discovers a fact adds something to the knowledge of the world.

"Why," I asked a spirit, "is knowledge not immediate and without process?"

"Because," was the reply, "knowledge is worth more when it is gained by self-effort. To every mortal who thinks rightly, Nature's laws become natural laws. It is only the ignorant who are blind to all that is going on around them. Each change in spirit-existence is partly hidden from the plane below, because the conditions of each change make it best for the soul to fit itself for the next, without absolute knowledge of the next step. All that is necessary is given to the soul when it is ready. As you, in earth-life, reach out for knowledge, much can be given to aid you to govern your earth-lives rightly, but not so much as to make you impractical in your daily work. Life in each sphere must be lived according to the laws of vibration that govern that sphere.

"When the right moment comes for the unfolding, the light breaks into the dark recesses of the mind, and the sudden radiance is dazzling. I keep telling you to live rightly and to teach others so to live. That is what earth-people must learn, but they are doing it very slowly. I tell you that the majority of souls on earth are sometimes centuries coming out of the deep shade of ignorance and sin. Learn to think good, pure, charitable thoughts. You cannot know the reward the future will bring."

IV. Progress

TO the average mind that has given no thought to the problem of life after this existence, and to its great possibilities, the suggestion that those out of-the body can communicate with us at all, is startling. The fact that any conditions have been made where they can speak in their own voice so as to be heard distinctly in our atmosphere, is beyond their comprehension. That spirit-people control the physical brain and hand to write, is beyond all understanding. The fact that millions of human beings have not heard or spoken to spirit-people, or seen them use the hand of a sensitive to write, does not even tend to prove that I have not had such experiences or that these are not facts. Knowledge is positive; ignorance is negative. I have seen the one and have heard the other again and again, and I know both to be facts; I have had taken down in writing many discussions and lectures on problems that are of vital interest. Let me give the words of a spirit on the subject of progress:

"In the great theatre of the universe all is harmony that pertains to the management of the play. The one touch of discord exists with players only. Gradually, but steadily, the players acquire a perfect knowledge of their various parts, and, as they learn to conduct themselves so as to allow the play to go on smoothly, the entertainment becomes more agreeable. But much rehearsing is required before a satisfactory exhibition can be given.

"That all who wish may enjoy that to which they are entitled is nature's full intent, and gradually mortals are coming to realize that such is the case. An appreciation of universal good for the benefit of mankind at large, can come only when the single and separate individual can clearly understand that he is entitled to those gifts of nature which his senses tell him may be had for the demanding. Until recently it was an almost universal belief that there were special privileges for a certain number of the supposed elect of God; but when a few who were barred out of those privileges, fearlessly raised their eyes and studied nature as it is presented on the stage of the universe, and learned that the only true supremacy and greatness lies in the difference of intelligence, and not in any distinction that can be marked by heredity, there came an awakening; and since that day, the scenes on the stage of your world have changed rapidly, and each succeeding one has shown an improvement over its predecessor. And when this appreciation of the only true mark of greatness among mortals has been realized, then and then only, will the cord of harmony be struck, and the play shall be so thrilling that the doors shall be open to the universe at large, and all the different constellations will ring with applause as they see one more evidence of the splendid work of the master mind.

"Knowledge is the key that shall open the door for this great production. Knowledge is the magic key to progress. With knowledge comes confidence; with confidence conies a strengthened desire for more knowledge. When the creeping babe first pulls its body to an erect position by its hands and arms, and finds that it can stand erect on its little feet, confidence in the power of its being is established, and the first forward movement of its feet gives it further knowledge of its power, and, as step by step, its feet carry forward its little body, knowledge of its power begets confidence, and confidence begets the possibility of acquiring further knowledge; and, until something occurs to weaken that condition, the forward and onward movement to acquire more knowledge is continued. As it is with the creeping, toddling child, so it is with the adult; until something occurs to stop that onward movement of gathering knowledge, progress is constant. What, then, is more terrible to contemplate than any system of teaching that can beget, or has begotten, fear, the great destroyer of confidence? Like one who sits upon a great height and has an unobstructed view of what is happening on the plains, we, of the spirit-world, can look with unobstructed vision down the long vista of the past, and see the terrible crimes that have been committed against our fellowspirits and earth mortals by those bands of men who dared to intimidate their fellow creatures, and to hold them in subjection by writing and preaching about things of which they were utterly ignorant. Some were mere fanatics; but in the main, they were mean, low, and unscrupulous men whose only thoughts were of personal gain and personal advantage. Awful will be the punishment of such men. Some are now undergoing their punishment in the spirit-world, and others are clinging tightly to those whom they have deceived, and, by suggestion, are still doing their harmful work."

When the intellect ceases to be enslaved, then is the body free. When knowledge holds full sway, then the intellect is free. Knowledge gives one the power of self-control, and when one has learned self-control, knowledge increases rapidly. And as one acquires knowledge, he gains self-control in like degree.

"Let fear and superstition and dread of the future be banished from the minds of men, so that they may see clearly and understand nature perfectly; then will knowledge come to them, imparted by those who have journeyed into the next stage of progress, the spiritual or stage of acute intelligence."

V. How Do I Know?

HOW do I know that individuality, personality, identity, and life itself, continue beyond the grave, and that the psychic world is about this world in what we know as space? If it is a fact, what method have I used to demonstrate it? Whether man lives after death is to science of more importance than how and where he lives. If the facts are finally accepted as I shall state them, then "what fools we poor mortals be" not to understand such a simple proposition! Let me ask these questions: (a) Do you know whether death is, or is not, the end? (b) Have you ever made any personal effort to find out? and (c) Do seventeen years of careful, earnest, intelligent work qualify one to speak?

I have only reached the noon of life; but, many years ago, not content that others should do my thinking, and unwilling to accept hearsay evidence, tradition and blind belief, I determined to discover the facts about the future life, if they were obtainable, and from those facts, draw my own conclusions.

The progress of the world has been so great that even the masses are coming to demand facts,—and facts that appeal to reason; less will not do. Have the great truths of nature been placed in the keeping of any class or set of men who alone are competent to explain? Or is the task left to any who seek truth in any guise? I long ago determined, having no preconceived notions, faiths or prejudices, and having at least nothing to unlearn, to devote such time to study and research on this subject as was possible. Furthermore, let me say that over twenty years in the active practice of law, largely in the trial of cases, coming in contact with many great minds, has qualified me to do certain things: i.e., to estimate the weight and value of evidence fairly; to detect fraud in any guise; to know when a fact is proved.

In conducting my experiments, I have always insisted that they should be done in my own home under such conditions only as I should provide. I use a room 10x14 feet, with windows opening to the west so that the evening sun will enter it daily, with shutters to break the rays of light and make it dark, when experimenting and working with psychic forces. Why work in the dark, do you ask? Because spirit-people, when they speak, must take on gross matter, must clothe their organs of respiration, or the voice would not vibrate in the material atmosphere. Light is motion; and so sensitive are they to light-waves that break down the material atoms with which they clothe themselves, that absolute darkness is a condition precedent, at least in my work, for them to speak. The room is remote from, and has no connection with any others; is so ventilated that the atmosphere is always pure; its only furnishings a carpet, chairs and a small table; its decorations are red—the warmest of colors—and here, with the aid of a psychic, I have year after year talked with those called dead.

Possessing no psychic powers myself, and such force being necessary to spirit speech, seventeen years ago I obtained the assistance of Mrs. Emily S. French, the finest psychic in the world to-day, and she has been a co-worker with me ever since. This splendid woman of culture and refinement, now 76 years of age, has, without compensation, devoted the evening of her life to aid me in solving the great problem of dissolution.

She contributes to the experiments such psychic force as is required, while I give the physical force that makes speech possible. Space will not allow me to go into the process used by spirit-people in taking on the material so that they can speak in our atmosphere; it is sufficient that they do. Remember, they have bodies of the same size, shape and contour as before; and, if clothed with gross matter, they can formulate and utter words just as well as when in this life. The question now is, do they speak, not how do they speak.

Mrs. French and I simply go into this room, already described, and sit in darkness, with the small table only between us.

The occasion is not solemn; nor are the surroundings gruesome; rather it is a school-room and the lecture hour devoted to the unfolding of nature's simple laws. Since I possess no psychic sight or hearing; what I hear must be material. Any can hear as I do. If, in this dark room, I see or feel anything, it is because the spirits have so reduced their vibration, so retarded, for the time, their atomic and molecular action, that they are, in fact, physical.

One morning, when Mrs. French and I were in this room talking to a physician who lived in the time of Alexander Hamilton and was one of his friends, a member of my family raised a window-shade in the attic, allowing sunlight to flash over the room. The rays were reflected through the ventilator in the ceiling, partially lighting the room directly over where a spirit-being stood talking. I saw his form perfectly; and, without a break in his discourse, he stepped to one side toward the corner where it was darker, continuing his discussion, simply saying as the place where he stood became partially lighted: "We have promised the time should come when you should see us, but we scarcely expected it would be this morning." He stood there in full materialized form, else how could I have seen him? He was a spirit, for Mrs. French and I were in the room alone, and no other man could have come in without opening the door and letting in the full light of day. I not only saw him, but I heard his spirit-voice, as I have heard it may times since. This is a fact: I saw, I heard, I know.

Physical demonstrations have never interested me. I have always wanted knowledge; and moving matter without application of physical force, granting it to be possible, has never appealed to me. I have had but few physical demonstrations. When Mrs. French and I were in this room some years ago, conversing with those in the planes beyond, I was told by one of my co-workers in spirit that they wanted to give me a test of their reality and power. Remember, Mrs. French and I were alone; the shutters were closed and the room was darkened; but outside the sun was shining. A spirit whose voice I recognized, said: "When I say 'now,' let Mrs. French stand, reach both her hands across the table, and you take hold of them firmly, regardless of what happens." The voice soon said, "Now." Mrs. French arose; I took both of her hands in mine, determined to hold them with great firmness, which I did, with senses keen in anticipation, but with no intimation of what was to happen. So firm was my hold on those hands that I knew, whatever happened, her hands could not aid in the demonstration. Soon the room was filled with the perfume of fresh flowers; one swished in the atmosphere and fell at my feet; my grip tightened on those frail hands; there was no movement of Mrs. French's body, but flowers came apparently from every direction, even from the ceiling, striking me on the head, face, chest, back and side, falling on the table and around us in great profusion. I immediately opened the door and hurriedly called others of my household to see the display. We found upon the table, chairs, and carpet, upwards of one hundred pure white sweetpeas, fresh, with dew sparkling in the petals. The stems had been twisted off.

At a later time, I asked how such a demonstration, so at variance with physical laws, was possible. I also asked whence came the flowers? I was told that no law had been violated, but that physical laws which mankind has not yet discovered, had been used; that spirit-people took sweet-peas from a garden where they grew in too great abundance, changed their vibratory condition, as we change water into steam, conveyed them in this state into the room, altered the vibration back again into its primary stage which restored the flowers to their original condition and color; then they threw them on and about me as I held Mrs. French's hands. This they did to show me their strength and to demonstrate a vibratory law. To this day I have kept some of those sweet-peas given by those spirit-people.

At other times when alone with Mrs. French, I have been told to take both her hands and to hold them firmly, during which time spirit-people have come in full physical form, stood beside me, and put their hands on my head. Their hands are warm and firm, but the touch is strange because they are in a state of intense vibration; they do not tremble or shake, but they seem to pulsate with a rapidity that I have not words to describe.

I can sit in this room with no one present but Mrs. French, one hand upon the table, her mouth on the back of that hand, my other hand on top of her head, holding it firmly so as to prevent the possibility of her speaking or moving her lips, and hear the spirit-people telling of life as they find it in the land of silence, as it is called.

At the demand of science, at one time, I permitted Mrs. French to go under test-conditions. They wanted to apply what is known as the "water-test that is, filling Mrs. French's mouth with water, to see if spirit-people could speak while she so held the liquid. At my request she consented. A man of science was chosen to make the experiment. He came and I gave him the key to the room in the afternoon, so that he might prepare his own conditions. In the evening, this learned professor, Mrs. French, and I, without lighting the room, and without any knowledge on our part of what condition it was in, entered. Mrs. French was given a certain quantity of liquid which this man put into her mouth. I could hear her breathe with difficulty. A moment's silence, and then a voice came in the darkness, unusually loud and strong, saying: "You see we can speak under the conditions you have made." I turned to the professor, asking: "Are you satisfied?" And he said: "I am." Then I said: "Remove the liquid; please measure it, and see if the amount expectorated is equal to the amount put in, and of the same color." I did not know the color or the amount. Upon examination, both were found intact. The test was evidential.

This man declined to publish this fact, saying it was in advance of the times. He was afraid that science, so-called, would not accept his statement. In view of such conditions I made arrangements some four years ago, for Mrs. French to go to New York at the request of Dr. Isaac Funk and his associates. She sat with him for eleven nights, the record of which is published in "The Psychic Riddle." Results similar to my own were obtained, and at a later time, Dr. Funk, at Rochester, applied the water-test again, and spirit-voices spoke to him while Mrs. French's mouth was filled with liquid. Such conditions demonstrate: (a) that Mrs. French does not do the talking, for her organs of speech are not used; (b) that the voices are independent. By that I mean that spirits use their own vocal organs.

Such facts convince me that people I have known in the body continue to live when the physical has gone back to dust, that they have the same individuality, the same continuity of thought, and the same characteristic speech in the after-life as in this.

By such experiments it is proved to be a fact that life continues after dissolution; that death is only a change of vibratory conditions; that the soul, mind, thought, by whatever name you chose to call this ego that thinks, reasons, and is, is in no way changed, only its action is governed by new laws controlling in the higher vibration of which they are a part They are the same persons as before; and, given the required conditions, can talk just as well as ever. This requires no deductive reasoning ; it is a fact proved and by many accepted.

One in spirit-life said to me, in discussing this subject this day:

"You know because you ask, and fact and reason answer. It is so even now, that few truths reach the intelligence of men which are not brought in wrappers of superstition, tied with baffling unreality. All creeds, founded on the little ambitions of a sect of men seeking their own renown, are being swept aside, and the truth, naked and unafraid, founded on nature's laws, is coming to be understood.

"Nature does not hide her laws, but holds them subject to the call of men, asking only that man shall qualify himself and know how to use and apply them intelligently, when they are unfolded to him. Nature is no miser, but is ever ready to give of her abundance."

VI. Spirit Identity

"HOW do I know," must be told on every page in different ways, but let us continue with the independent voice, for, in the history of the world as written, and as spirit-people tell me, never before has such freedom of speech been known; never before have spirit-people of a high order of intelligence found an avenue of communication with the physical world so effectual. How could it be more convincing than by voice to voice? My work has ever been conducted with great care and caution; every known safeguard has been adopted. I have never sought fraud, and have never found fraud; have ever sought truth, and have always found truth. A man's mind is like a magnet and the thought-waves emanating into the ether, attract waves of like character.

The key to the after-life is passivity, not concentration. By centering the mind on some particular thing much desired, the thought waves are contracted, brought to a slower vibration. Spirit-people in higher atomic activity, cannot come into a mental condition pulsating at a slow rate; but into the passive mind where the waves are more active, more nearly in harmony with a spirit's vibratory condition. So we talk for a few moments preceding spirit-speech on general matters, filling the room with vocal vibrations which are taken up and used by spirit-people,—our thoughts intent on no particular subject or person. When we meet to continue our investigations, a period of ten to twenty minutes elapses before spirit-people speak, during which time I feel as though some great power was in some indefinite way drawing upon my physical strength, at times almost to the point of pain; then the hush of expectancy; then the greeting, as in any drawing room, and quite as natural, as they come in one by one.

Working on the spirit-side of life, aiding this work, was originally a group of seven persons, who built up conditions every time we conducted experiments, the most important of which is the chemist, for he must know at once what conditions will harmonize, and what elements can be used and applied to different spirits to enable them to use their organs of speech so that their voice will reach our ears. We contribute, as I have said, physical vibrations, while spirit-people bring spiritual, that is a higher vibratory state, which the group manipulates. The condition under which we get these voices, is a utilization of both.

Certain of the spirit-group arrange these requisite conditions, while others direct the work. In the beginning of my investigations, the voices came usually in whispers, the people speaking were generally persons of less than the average intellect, those in the lower walks of life; such characters predominated, and the most we could get from them was the conditions in which they found themselves,—interesting, but not particularly instructive, as they had little knowledge of life beyond the earth plane. It was all, I see now, that we were able to comprehend; but our progression was to be commensurate with our capacity. Year by year, as we grew more accustomed to the work, and more able to understand these higher laws, there was improvement, until now the finest minds of modern times devote their time to our instruction. From the ungrammatical speech of ordinary men and women, step by step, it has changed to the finest diction, the most splendid English to which I have ever listened; and it is our privilege to enjoy, night after night, oratory finer than was ever delivered from any platform. Is it any wonder that I find such work intensely interesting, and have the courage born of knowledge to give the world what I have learned?

So mighty is the force of human thought, and so delicate are the conditions of a spirit's body when it has taken on material in preparation for speech, that, by word of command, or even by thought-projection, I can break down its conditions and prevent speech. This is why those who oppose this philosophy so often get negative results when they seek demonstration; by their mental attitude or thought-conditions, they make impossible the very thing they seek; they so intensify their thought-substance that spirit-people are not able to break into the conditions they make for the occasion.

Here is another piece of evidence which proves that the voices are not those of mortals: Spirit-people in speech with me, while using their organs of respiration, do not breathe as we do. I have often heard a lecture twenty minutes in length, without a break, the voice rising and falling in inflection, speaking with great force and clearness, but not drawing one breath in all that time. This is a physical impossibility for any mortal man.

Each voice has individuality. When a new spirit comes for the first time and takes on the condition of vocalization, there is often a similarity in tone quality, but this soon passes away, as they grow accustomed to using their voices in this way. The voices of those accustomed to speak, never change, and are easily recognized. Of such we never ask their names, for we know. There is no similarity of thought or words; these differ in different people in that world as in this.

The strength of the voices varies greatly; one of our group speaks with sufficient volume to fill easily a great auditorium, and his lectures ring through the whole house. Another whom I have in mind, always comes with great dignity and courtesy, is careful in speech and considerate; but his voice, while very distinct, has not great volume. The voice of another, who was very near to me in earth-life, is as clear, strong, and natural as in the days when we discussed this philosophy, or walked in the forest trying to understand and come in touch with the law of life; and we have since his going talked as much, and with as great freedom, as in the latter years before his going. There has been no subject of knowledge common to us both, that he ever hesitated to discuss in all its minutest details. This friendship of many years is continued without a break, and I enjoy his presence and our talks as I never did before.

One night, a voice of great volume and strength came out of the darkness, clothing thoughts with such speech as only one man has ever used, telling of life as he, who was one of the world's great agnostics, found it after dissolution; of his life-work and duties there, and something of the environment of a spirit and the possibilities of progression, closing by saying, "I am Mr. G.," as we will call him.

I said to Mr. G.: "It is one of the rules, long in practice in our work, that when one comes as you have, teaching philosophy, identity shall be proved. Can you do this?" He said: "I think that can be done without difficulty." I replied: "Did you ever meet me?" He said: "Yes." "Where?" I asked. "At the Niagara Hotel in your City." "When was that?" He said: "I don't recall the year, but it was when I gave a lecture on Progress at the request of the Beal Estate Men's Association." "What was the date of that lecture?" He replied: "I don't now recall, but it was in the early nineties." "Where was the meeting?" "At Music Hall, as I now recall." "Do you remember who sat in the box at your left that evening?" "My recollection is," he replied, "that my wife and daughter did, with others." *This was proof; it was all true.* This is one of the ways adopted to prove identity; and this man stood the test to my entire satisfaction.

Another instance: In my early work, in fact one of the first times I attempted to have speech with spirit, Mr. K., we will call him, was with me. He was one of those men who are always looking for tests, it was his ruling passion. He wanted tests more than he did knowledge, and as we were not seeking the same thing, we soon went different ways; but, whenever he met me, not having the courage of his desire, he would whisper: "Have you had any tests lately?" Whenever I saw him coming I knew what his question would be. So he lived, and so he died; and within a week, out of the darkness came a voice in greeting. I said: "Who is it, please? Can you tell us who you are? Give us something that will establish your identity. Can you?" "Yes," he replied, "I am through looking for tests."

One evening one spoke who said he was a physician of Philadelphia, and was brought in that help might be given to complete the separation from his physical body. When he finally became fully conscious, he told his name, the number of his residence, and much about himself.

The papers the next morning had a full account of his death early the evening before.

Mr. N., we will call him, was one of the most prominent members of our bar. lie was supposed to be in perfect health, but late one evening he was found dead. I had no knowledge of the circumstances. He told me his name and proved his identity without the slightest difficulty, for I had known him intimately. He asked me to send word to his brother, of New York, who, he said, was then in Europe—a fact I did not know—and told me where he himself was and what he was doing when dissolution came. The circumstances were verified by his son at a later time. Space forbids detail. I have mentioned only a few out of thousands of similar cases.

In the beginning, much time was wasted to prove the identity of strange spirits who were allowed to talk, to find if what they said concerning themselves, was true; and while I know that spirit-people, as a rule, are as prone to deceit as mortals, I recall no instance of it. At one time, few men of my acquaintance passed on who did not come and speak with me; but now the strength is so limited, owing to the great age of our psychic, that personal interviews are not frequent, the time being used in giving information concerning this great problem and teaching this new philosophy, that the greatest good may come to the greatest number.

Hundreds, yea thousands, have come and talked to me, and to many whom I have invited to participate in the work,—thousands of different voices with different tones, different thoughts, different personalities, no two alike; and at times in different languages.

Spirit identity is a subject I have always considered important for many reasons: (a) It may be said, if a spirit can prove identity, that it is evidence that life continues; (b) by knowing who he is, his education, experience and opportunity for observation, one can tell what weight to give his teachings, for, as I have pointed out elsewhere, spirit-people differ concerning many great questions just as people do in this life, and we must ever exercise our reason and draw our own conclusions. That is the way character is developed. Every statement made and every alleged fact that comes to us from either world, must be tested in the crucible of reason and must appeal to our common sense, before it can be accepted; and unless it comes from the retort pure, we discard it.

No spirit ever feels at liberty to come into our sessions without the invitation of the spirit-group or of myself any more than a stranger would come into my house for social purposes without an invitation. The same laws of privilege and hospitality which operate in the earth-life, prevail in the spirit-world.

There is opposition to this work in spirit-spheres just as in this. The Catholic Church exists as an institution in the afterlife, and is just as jealous of its domination as it is here. In our earliest work these opponents often tried to prevent speech by interrupting and disorganizing the conditions we sought to maintain, fearing that the truth might cause loss of temporal as well as spiritual power; and great efforts were made by the spirit-group, comprising our co-workers, to control and maintain the conditions, and to keep them out. I recall one evening when my stenographer was taking a lecture in shorthand, that a Catholic spirit gained admittance; and such was his material strength that he suddenly wrenched the stenographic book from the hands of the stenographer, and threw it with great violence against the wall of the room. Our group finally forced him out and, as he was leaving, I heard him say, rWhat can one man do among so many millions?"

VII. Of Many Minds

THE greatest fallacy of the human race is the belief that people, after dissolution, know everything, or that they agree, upon great propositions, any more than in this life. There is absolutely nothing in metaphysics to warrant such a foolish assumption. Nothing in the world is acquired without effort, and there is no evidence that the scheme of nature is changed by what is known as death. Those who hold that through the change from the physical to the spiritual men become gods, know very little about evolution, and wrongly assume that there is one law for the physical and another for spirit-life. The fact is, all nature's laws are universal, and apply alike to both planes, for, to some extent, both occupy the same space. This being so, we can appreciate the wisdom of creation and that it is worth while, if one continues his life and work beyond the physical, to acquire all possible knowledge and development while living in the physical plane, to the end that he may be better equipped when going beyond it.

Dissolution is a step in evolution, and involves no mental change, adding nothing, subtracting nothing, but simply increasing the opportunities for observation and learning. As men regard this subject with so much indifference, it is easy to conceive how overpowering will be the situation presented when separated from the physical body: no going away; no flight to the sky; no sudden acquisition of knowledge; no personal God; but self in a new light, in a true light; many of the so-called dead rushing to meet the newcomer as he takes the little step out of this life, into spirit-existence, while, as his eyes open, and the truth flashes upon his dull senses, he discovers that God is Universal Good, which has been, and is, the dominant factor both in the physical and spirit-plane; that this force for good has held kingship since the world began; that man has been, and ever will be, a part of that force, increasing the sum total of that power of which he is a part, according to the measure of his progression! This he does by developing the atom of good that he became at the moment of his conception. It came from that great force of Universal Good; and, let him go to and fro as he will, yet, drawn by an irresistible force, he will return to the goal from which he came originally; and, inasmuch as there is some good in everyone, the sum-total of that force for good will be enriched to some extent by his return. But this will not come at the moment of dissolution, for that is only one step along the way, and no matter though he live in the body beyond his allotted time, his life is practically only just beginning.

When dissolution is past, and one has paid all his obligations to the physical world, (no progression being possible until this is done, for nature's laws are terrible in their exactness), and realizes his condition, the necessary thing is to take an inventory of his equipment, and to determine how far he is qualified to assume the duties and responsibilities awaiting him. He may be a great lawyer, an eloquent divine, a great financier, a learned professor, a good merchant, or an honest farmer; but how will that help him when he is spirit dealing with matter in so high a state of vibration that it no longer resists muscular effort, the existence of which he has never before known? How will such a man deal with conditions of which he is so densely ignorant and which control his every thought and movement? There is but one answer: he must form new conceptions based on known facts and necessities, and, aided by the limited knowledge that he has acquired, he must commence again, commence, at best, where dissolution overtook him; the better equipped here, the more advanced there. When I say equipped, I do not mean with material knowledge, but with a broad comprehension of natural laws; this alone will aid one in adapting himself to the environment in the new community of which he has become an inhabitant.

In this material world of ours there are many opinions on every great subject; each works to a conclusion from known facts, but the conclusions arrived at are not always correct. Spirit-people hold to their opinions after dissolution until they are changed by the new facts presented. They do not agree on many great questions any more than we do. They fail to understand many of nature's laws as mortals do, and are continually laboring to come to a better knowledge of them just as we do here; and there, as here, are "many minds," but as to what immediately follows dissolution all agree.

The fact that spirit-people, though advanced and learned in many ways, greatly differ on many subjects, was impressed on my mind by one in the after-life while discussing the subject of "sound", when he said:

"One of the facts that has been repeatedly proved by experiment, is that the stress-condition, which I have heretofore referred to, is an existing condition, that when a blow is struck upon various kinds of substance, a very widely differing sound is produced, and that the distinctive notes are, of course, the resulting vibration of the particular mass struck.

"It is not, to me, a satisfactory explanation that the sound that reaches our ear is only the result of the elasticity of the particles of the mass acting strictly among themselves, the vibration of the mass itself and, also, the vibration of the particles of the mass; but, the true solution of the problem is, I think, and many agree with me, that the blow upon the mass may bring the particles of the mass momentarily to a state of rest, and so the mass itself may be temporarily reduced to a similar state, or both the particles and the mass composed of the particles may be, for and during the period of the concussion, rendered, so to speak, physically dead,—this phenomena being based on the fact that all matter is in constant vibratory motion. And now, granting my hypothesis that all matter produces in the surrounding ether a state of stress, the mirrored condition of its actual self, I think it necessarily follows that if the actual substances were brought to a momentary state of rest, the lines of existing stress reaching out from the object struck, would, on the instant, feel the effect, and the something called sound would be the result of their sudden interference, and the prolongation of the apparent sound would depend upon the length of the period of the suspension of the actual vibration of the object struck.

"This and many other facts lead others on this side of life to advocate the stress-theory. And again, there are many very well informed men on this side of life who argue against such a theory."

"When this matter was brought to the attention of such on this side of life as are interested along these lines, much discussion occurred, and it is, and has been, argued from two viewpoints: first, as simply impossible; and second, as reasonable, if the theory of existing stress, in the ether surrounding known substances, be logical. All of those trying to assist you, hold the latter."

Such discussions impress one with the reality and earnestness of the people beyond, and show how they labor to comprehend all natural law.

VIII. Speech With Spirit-People

TO the end that all may better comprehend the character of the teaching that has been given me from time to time, I quote from the speech of many spirit-people on different subjects, as it was recorded at the time:-

"A new branch of literature, relating wholly to the laws of psychic phenomena, is just entering the cycle of progressive thought. Let no experiment be unrecorded; your material is valuable. Every idea promulgated will be of universal interest."

"The supreme need for each man is to reason, and to remain, ever after, true to his convictions. Where reason leads, you must follow publicly and openly. This is the highest conception of duty."

"Men who deny to others the right of public speech are not qualified for speech themselves. Men criticize things they have not mastered, and do not understand."

"Why are old experiences repeated? you ask. Because the tangle of life must be made right, and it must be made right by the individual soul. This is the truth I taught. Only a few are ready for it, and even to-day only a few enter into my sphere. There are those in earth-life with whom I daily and hourly commune; there are those here who still seek expression through some form of earthly religious belief; *few are willing to stand alone and think.*"

"Nature is an open book, with language simple and easy to comprehend; yet man, with all his boasted knowledge, has read but few pages and mastered less. Its lessons are written in rocks, in earth, in minerals and grasses, in grains, in flora, in trees, in bursting bud and growing things, in mountains, in snows and glaciers, in sun and stars, and in all movement and evolution of matter, gross and refined."

"I believe a man's conscience is his judgment-seat; and that reparation for wrong cannot begin too soon. I believe that love for humanity is the basis upon which mankind must stand to gain ultimate good;

that to help a sprawling beetle to gain its feet is an act the result of which will follow one through eternity."

"Beyond the great divide, await all those for whom you mourn; all unsatisfied ambitions, providing they are tending toward progression, you will have the power to gratify, by work and application."

"We belong to a vast army of workers; whose work consists in developing the best that is in us, both as individuals and collectively. Our souls must be developed on a large scale, so as to include all humanity, and, until we have this largeness in our souls, our work for ourselves progresses but slowly. It is the feeling of universal oneness that makes us great individually."

"Brood well upon that with which you store your mind. Each grain of knowledge will grow and bear its fruit."

"Literature, art, all the great work of masters, all the products of the genius of the present and the past, will come to the assistance of those who call. We are here to aid, to comfort, to uplift and to support all who ask for help. Only a few here have a faint glimpse of a life beyond the satisfaction of earth-desires. Like tendrils clinging to a wall or to a decaying tree, through disappointed loves and blasted hopes, they keep tenaciously struggling with the problem of mortal life."

"Open your eyes and you shall see the new heaven and the new earth, all invisible to the physical eye, which sees only that which it wants to see, but it sees nothing of the eternal harmony, of which mortals express only a counterpart. Awake to the truth of the joy of being! Awake to the infinite cause of all happiness! Awake to the omni-active energy that surrounds you!"

"All beauty is expression in a varied language—not of words, but of pure ideas, hopes and joys. Emotions have a language not yet comprehended, and yet to be given to a listening, waiting, longing world. Be filled with joy! That is the expression of God. If you would impress your thought on others, and spread the truth, make that thought the highest expression of truth! Make your life a continual song of thanksgiving for the good you find, and the good you give to others. Be consistent, looking to the harmony of natural law to guide you, and build your life on the same sim-pie principle. This life means to the true thinkers a wondrous unfolding, beginning with a child's first conscious look, going on and on until the individual is taken into the one great scheme of indivisible good. This is the ultimate end of all."

"The universe is teeming with life,— beautiful, abundant life. Open your soul and stretch out as it were with eager hands, and let the spirit of Good enter, and abide. Like dew upon a thirsty, famished flower, it will make a sick soul well. It is the same force that is in the dew; only to the flower it must come in the form of *dew, rain* or *shine; while to mankind it comes as a suggestion,* enters into the mind, makes it strong and courageous; for a mind filled with the uplifting principle, which is Good, must be a pure one, one able to lead others to the great book of nature, there to learn to obey its laws—laws steadily, insistently, working for each blade of grass, each soul of man."

"Beware of criticism. It kills naturalness in yourself and others, and the best impulses are suppressed by the frost of self-criticism. Attune yourself to the most harmonious vibrations, so that your impulses will be good, and then obey them. They are apt to be the suggestions of a fellow-soul working out his salvation; and, by letting the impulse hold sway over you, you not only do a good act, but help that struggling soul one step farther on his way."

"When the end drew near and I knew my judgment was at hand, my spirit shuddered with horror. I knew I had not lived according to divine good. I had deceived, and, more than that, I had lied and abused the confidence of many who looked up to me. Will I ever be able to complete the restitution necessary? Sometimes my soul sickens under the burden of sorrow and suffering I have caused, and I am afraid. I want, by these teachings which I am privileged to give you, to gain much for my own advancement. Perhaps you and I together may grow in greater harmony each day so that much good may come of it. Call me when you will, I will be watching, eager to take up the work."

IX. Thought And Mind

THERE are certain expressions and sentences in our language which are, at present, substantially meaningless, because the mind is unable to grasp what it cannot analyze. That "thought is substance" and "mind is matter," mean but little to mortal man, notwithstanding his wonderful progress, because so little is known of matter outside of and beyond that which resists muscular effort, or which he cannot observe with his physical eyes.

Those that are educated along material lines see only in earth, water and air, certain atoms, molecules and chemical combinations. All must admit that matter is governed by force, and that the force that governs and directs matter in its association, composition and change, possesses intelligence; but, being unable to follow matter through its evolution and refinement, they deny what they cannot comprehend. Back of the atom, back of all substance, back of all people, is a mighty force, called mind,—-the Master Mind we may term it, that directs and controls all substances visible and invisible by fixed and definite rules, which are termed "natural law".

To attempt to bring to the comprehension of mankind a definite conception of that mind, that force, is difficult beyond anything I have undertaken, because of my limited knowledge of the subject; for those in the sphere beyond the physical are able to give me but little information, for they have only limited knowledge. Simply because they are out of the body they do not know all, nor are they infallible ; so they, acting as instructors, can give me only that which they know. Perhaps I can deal with this difficult proposition in no better way than to quote what spirit-people have told me concerning the question.

"Back in the past centuries, when the world of spirit had not its present development, there was little original inventive thought. Man built a shelter, killed his food, and fought his enemies, as any animal does. As the spirit-world progressed, and became more intelligent; as it obtained greater understanding, and grasped, with greater power, the life-forces, or, in other words, more power of thought and more ability to help mortal development, then, by reason of spirit-suggestion, acting through man's sub-conscious mind, he began to feel an awakening for something better and the progress of civilization began."

This statement emphasizes the fact that all life in every sphere ever has been, now is, and ever shall be, progressive; that there was a time in spirit-planes, as well as on this, when they did not possess the intelligence, comprehension and power that they do to-day, nor nearly as much as they will in time to come.

Of what lies beyond the next, or first spirit-sphere, those who live there know but little. Knowledge is acquired only by effort, there, as here; and only as we comprehend the economy of natural law and mindpower, do we progress. We know that those in the next spirit-sphere, like people in the earth-sphere, develop their mental powers through acquired knowledge, and therefore, increase the sum-total of the Master-Mind of which they and we are parts; so that not only is the individual spirit gaining advancement, but being Spirit, and a component part of the great Mind, this force increases in the ratio of individual development; each day they and we are contributing something to the great intelligent force which directs and controls the Universe; and its increase is measured by their and our progression.

What the Master-Mind is, beyond the fact that it includes the individual minds of all who have lived, and now live, in any plane or any planet in the universe, we cannot know; we could not grasp the Infinite, if any spirit knew and tried to explain. That there is an intelligence controlling all matters and all people to some extent, we do know.

Again this spirit said:

"Beyond and before everything is mind; that is, understanding. Mind is matter, as you use that term, with this difference; it is carried beyond the physical into a higher vibration. Let me illustrate in this way: good thoughts have a higher and more rapid vibration than bad thoughts, and bring us into closer harmony with spirit-intelligences. There is no barrier to thought; it carries us to the uttermost parts of the earth; to the heights of perfect joy and to the depths of woe. The people of earth are just beginning to gain some knowledge of this force for good within themselves. Once let that fact be understood, and mortals will come nearer to understanding their destiny."

Another said:

"Mind is the aggregate of all thoughts. Mind is the universal thought. As a drop of water signifies but one infinitesimal part of the great ocean, so a thought is but one infinitesimal part of the great ocean of mind. *Thought is creative energy, the essence of all things, and expresses itself in form.* The vibratory energy of thought-waves produce form, sound and color, though they are never perfectly expressed in the physical plane. Not until men have arisen out of the physical condition can they come to an appreciation and comprehension of matter so refined as to be known as mind. *Thought belongs to the individual man; mind to the race universal.*"

Words are but symbols used to express thoughts. There is nothing in a word except that it conveys an impression or ideas to the mind. They are coined as new conditions arise. When Newton discovered the law of gravitation, he had difficulty in finding words to describe the fact, so new was the proposition. So it is with metaphysics, that is the philosophy of life beyond the physical; this science is so new and so little is known on the subject, that words have not as yet been adopted that will allow of exact detail or comprehensive report.

There is no such thing as space; what seems so to us, in fact, contains all the elements that produce objects, but it is so fine in its particles and in so high a state of vibration as not ordinarily to be visible. All in the earth and sky is substance and holds within itself life force. The wind is matter, for we feel it in our faces, and is a force for it drives great ships upon the seas. Water is slower in vibration than atmosphere, so we feel and see it, while ether, which is atmosphere higher in vibration, we neither see nor feel, yet it permeates all things and all space and is likewise a substance.

I said to a spirit who in earth-life, was the foremost scientist of his time, "What is ether?" and what is mind?" and he answered:

"Ether is simply atmosphere in more intense vibration than that which surrounds the earth. Ether surrounds spirits unless they go into the earth-plane. Mind, I mean the thought, not the habitation of thought, when the earth-life is over, becomes the entire being. It is the only part in man that is of such vibration that it can enter in and progress to spirit-life. The brain is so constructed that there is an opening for spirit-force or suggestion; consequently, it proves that the entire mind is of such vibration that the spirit-force can reach it; otherwise suggestion would be impossible.

Mind is the essence of being,—the ego. It is material, but differing in vibration from the body. Spirit-force surrounds the flowers, teaching them how to grow and bloom, but they have no .*conscious original thought*.

And so we find matter rising higher and higher in vibratory action. First the earth, then water, then atmosphere, then ether, and finally, mind, which is matter as much as the earth is matter, yet it directs and controls all substance in a lower vibratory condition.

Let me illustrate: Over the land that a man owns, and the waters under the land, he has some control. He can dig into the earth; he can draw the water from it; he can use the air and, to some slight degree, deflect its currents, by the mind directing hands and other agencies that he can employ. He holds *limited* dominion over gross matter under certain conditions. Now, spirit-minds, that make up the Master-Mind, higher in vibration than ether itself, hold absolute dominion over all matter in the physical universe. But, to attempt to analyze that Master-Mind, or one's own mind even, to give the component parts of mind-matter or its chemical composition, is beyond my power.

One of my spirit co-workers said:

"Be tempted to one extravagance only in this book of ours. Use every argument and all the forcefulness you can, to show what a little thing, what a tiny span, the earth-life is. Real life begins when the heavy, material body is left behind, and the soul springs upward into the unlimited regions of thought-life. There all grows, learns, expands into perfect fullness of being until one becomes a perfectly developed spirit, able to blend with other spirits similarly developed and perfected. There is no beginning and no end, then, to the heights he can ascend; no joy that is unknown or untasted; no wonder of the universe of which he does not become a part. It is being, then, that state which cannot be defined to unthinking and uncomprehensive minds. But try to grasp this idea, for it gives such an interest and zest to every-day life. Some day each shall be a part of the great force that makes all things work in unity. Before the force was so strong, there was not so much good working among men. They were cruel, barbarous and uncontrolled. Much has that mind-force, working silently but constantly, achieved in the past ages, and much more will it achieve, now that mankind has become more receptive to our suggestion."

"Thought is the expression of mind; it is partly caused by spirit-suggestion through the sub-conscious mind, and partly an expression of oneself. Deeds are thoughts grown to maturity, and yet a thought unspoken or unlived, will exist through all the ages, as though expressed."

X. Nature's Laboratory

ALL the universe is the result of chemical action; this entire earth, and all upon it, is one great laboratory wherein nature's forces are ever active, controlled by laws made and kept in operation by the Master Intelligence.

Nature abhors inaction and stagnation; life-force permeates every atom that goes to make up the mass which we call earth. We call the activity and expression of that force, energy. The ceaseless effort of this force to obtain development, coming into touch with other chemical conditions in nature's wonderful retort, is a refining process, working for the advancement of mankind. An interesting discussion on this subject by a spirit is as follows:

"It should appeal to you that each atom, or each element, and each molecular aggregation of sub-atoms, must possess distinct individuality. The scheme of nature, so far as so-called inanimate matter is concerned, is to allow a perfect expression of the individual characteristics of each separate species. The individual expression of those separate kinds of matter, be it in the atom or in that expression of associate atoms that produce separate effects, is to allow the steady and ever-occurring change that matter is constantly undergoing to bring about progressive conditions. As matter is ever undergoing a process of refinement in the great laboratory, it follows that, inasmuch as the rule must be an all-including one (for no exception is allowed by nature) a period of time must come when the material of which the human brain is fashioned will also be effected by the refining process.

"The time has arrived when this effect on the mortal brain is being observed by men, for the brain of the present day has reached the most sensitive stage in the world's history. Being thus attuned, by the gradual and ever-active process of refinement of matter, it is quickened in vibratory power, and thus is in more perfect accord with the vibratory activity of the people of the next step in progression, those who live without the clothing of the flesh. It is possible, also, for some few physical beings to be held in mental accord by certain spirit-people. The refined physical brain can adjust itself to the spirit-brain, so that the latter can dictate to the former comprehensive suggestions as to the proper method of procedure to grasp, harness, and control those subtle, magnetic forces of fixed, ever-existing, steady, but pulsating, conditions of stress that are the perfect reflex of the ever active particles of matter.

"It is a well established fact, that substances of the same kind attract each other and are cohesive in a given mass in so-called solid form, by a reduction of temperature. This kind of attraction has no relation to chemical attraction, but is mainly based on the physical characteristics of the substance, made possible by the similarity of the crystalization of the substance. Much has been told and explained to you about this subject of crystalization of substance. It is the true demonstration of the acute individuality of distinct elements and positive (actual) substance. As vegetablisin and animalism assert their different species by the process just referred to, so all things in the world of matter likewise assert themselves.

"Different species of the vegetable and animal kingdom, by the fact of distinct crystalization (form), possess the power to give expression to all the fixed and distinct peculiarities that they possess, and to effect others of their kind, or of similar species, and mix and become assimilated with each other in their progressive action, and thus assert that subtle influence which you know as perpetuating life; the one nutrifying the other. Thus they give expression to that power, which is the deep-seated principle of nature, that you explain *as life, and that we know is the Spirit.* So also is it with matter. It is permeated with Spirit Life, and, because of that fact, it is ever-active. If it were not for this fact, that it possesses Spirit or Life, matter could not undergo the ever-occurring changes, all of a progressive character, that it does; it could not change to unite and form substances and, after these new combinations have performed their duties, to break down and form some other substances which also fulfil their functions in the progression of nature's great scheme. Were the atoms dead, spiritless, they would of necessity be non-active, and hence useless for the work of the Master's hand.

"Matter, gross or fine, is but a vehicle for the use of the Spirit, and be it the invisible, theoretical atom of oxygen or of any other so-called element, or be it a perfect physical man, this atom of matter, or these aggregations of atoms used to form man, are but the Master's vehicles to work for, and act as the carrier of, the Spirit. *The Spirit of man is the intelligence of man} and nothing more. This Spirit* is the highest type that the Master has desired to create on your earth. It is the consummation of the workmanship of that great workshop, your earth; and it is the final result of the activity of all other spirit-forces that matter has for countless ages, as man records time, been manifesting.

"The final product of all of that ceaseless activity of matter is the one result that goes out from your earth as Eternal Life. Every other form of spirit-life is returned to the refinery for the further processes of refinement, until it is fitted for the last act of earth-life,—the creating of a sublime human intelligence,—and then it goes forth into the domain of Spirit, to be further refined and fitted for that purpose of the Master *that is not clear to us of the Spirit World,* but, according to reasoning, based on such knowledge as is possessed by some of our most advanced intelligences, to be ultimately a power added to the great Intelligence that rules the universe. But be the further following out of the scheme what it may, of this truth you may be certain: God's use of this earth is to create human intelligence; and further, it is nature's constant effort to produce the best; and, so true is this, that, if you will but "read" as you "run," you may note that people of your earth possess this knowledge as if by instinct (in reality by spirit-suggestion) and they are constantly endeavoring, in their blind, groping way, to perfect themselves. Thus likewise it is with spirit-people.

"Clearly we see, clearly we feel, all that you see and all that you feel. As your sensations are the half-blind groping of a lower organism, sluggish, and dull as to the true facts that underlie real progress; so ours are the quick, clear, and fully-developed faculties for appreciating great truths. This refers only to those spirit-intelligences among us who have been awakened to a complete appreciation of our actual individual spirit intelligence, or, plainly, to those among us who have come to realize our complete separation from the physical body after dissolution has occurred. We are as much John Smith or Wilhelm Schneider in the spirit-life as when in the flesh, and we have the same distinct personalities.

"Thus, knowing by quick perception, as we do, that only right is right, and that deception cannot succeed; that honesty only is a fact, and that dishonesty is a condition that brings about endless trouble that must be disentangled and made straight and absolutely honest by the causer; and, knowing that nature has established laws which are good, and, if adhered to, beneficial in their results; and which, if broken, must be mended by the breaker,—knowing all these things made possible by our power of rapid perception, (because those tantalizing desires of the flesh have no longer a hold upon us) we are ever and always anxious when we can come in touch with intelligence in the flesh, to give to such persons what we can of the truths that are clear to us."

XI. Vibration

SCIENCE can measure the velocity of the wind, of the stars and constellations, and of rays of light; but who shall attempt to measure the velocity of human thought? We cannot demonstrate spirit-forces and the conditions governing them, by the same rules that are applied to physical science. This is simply because there is a difference in the rate of vibration between things material and things spiritual. As long as matter is sensible to touch, science can measure it, analyze its substance, and learn its component parts; but when it reaches a certain vibration, where activity increases beyond their knowledge, the "scientists" are lost in the wilderness which they call "the unknown." This is where the philosophy that we term "metaphysics" commences. We, of this new school of thought, are no more qualified to enter into the domain of physical science than the physical scientists are to come into our domain, and it would be most profitable for each school to confine itself to its own field of usefulness.

Sir William Thompson, led by a hint of Faraday's, advances the theory that "all properties of matter, probably, are attributes of motion." I am told there are but two elements in the universe. This must be so: the positive and the negative, male and female; else how could we have the harmony of the universe, and the tendency to final equilibrium of inharmonious conditions and things. All other conceivable elements are not elements, but compounds. Vibrations are slowest in the basic or generic rocks; the atoms and molecules composing them lying close, of necessity, movement is slow. The basic rock, where it has not been changed in its position by upheavals, is most removed from the earth's surface. It has changed but little from the condition it assumed when this planet cooled and substance came together in so-called solids; but, starting from this generic rock as our basis of comparison, as we come up through the different strata in which are recorded the earth's ages, we observe the vibration gradually quickening as matter changes in its formation, resulting in greater motion; the vibrations intensify as we reach the soil and growing grains and trees, the plants and shrubs, and, finally, the flowers, bringing motion up to the highest pitch in the vegetable kingdom. But vibrations do not cease there; as we reach man they increase. After the physical comes the spirit-body, still matter, still vibrating, which progresses on and on among spirit-spheres with ever increasing action, in spirit-planes, its refining process never ceases increasing, any more than man ceases progressing.

Vegetation has life, the same character or kind of life as human beings, but, its vibration being slower, it cannot move of its own volition. The only thing that makes it possible for man to move at will, is because he is in a higher or more rapid state of vibration, but with movement limited,—for all things have their limitations. We cannot pass through solids; but spirit-people, living in a higher state of vibration, can. The spirit, while in the body, whose vibrations are slower and heavier, is impeded in its movement by the material; but at dissolution it escapes physical impediments, its molecular or atomic action increases, and it can do more at will. There is quite as much difference between the vibration in and out of the body as between the physical body and vegetable kingdom. Dissolution, then, is only the changing of vibratory conditions. It has been illustrated to me in this way:

"When the body, from disease or long inhabitation, becomes a broken shell, the intense vibration of the spirit breaks through the limiting space to which it has become accustomed, and reaches a plane of higher vibration. The soul-sense dominates all our thoughts and actions; and, consequently, it is held in check only by the physical limitations of the body. When, as I say, the body becomes unfit to hold the spirit, the spirit breaks away at the first opportunity, and seeks the sphere best adapted for its expansion. The heavy vibrations of the body, unless quickened by the presence of the keener soul-vibrations, fall back into the still heavier vibrations of matter, which is earth and no vegetation. Nothing remains stationary, and if one part goes onward, the other goes backward. These are the elementary laws that govern change and evolution, and they are the A B C of spirit-knowledge. As this is becoming more known among those in earth-life, it tends toward their ultimate benefit."

"There are always vibrations depending upon the subjection of molecules that are not so free in expression. I mean they are taken into the life-principle, and given their proper position; they change only to go into the vibration that is gradually made for them. They do not have the sudden release that comes to the soul, but slowly glide from one form into another, all in the same series of vibratory action. The soul's change is usually so sudden as to be a shock; for it is hard for a spirit to accustom itself to the intenser vibration. This is the reason why at a death-bed there is always a gasping for breath. It is not the physical body that is striving to breathe; it is the soul, emerging into that higher atmosphere of spirit, unconsciously trying to adjust itself."

"Spirit-material is only earthly matter raised to a higher degree of atomic activity. Chemistry shows that when two elements, having a different degree of atomic motion, come together, there is an attempt at equilibrium, which, being accomplished, produces a new form of matter, and in the spirit-world there is no change of law."

In the progress of matter from the simplest elemental state to the most complex organic compound, there is constantly (a) increase in the mass, (b) decrease in the stability of the molecules. This is well known in physical science, but a new condition is discovered: (c) with all these changes there is an increase in the activity of the properties which continues, not only as long as matter is sensible to touch, but through all the planes of life beyond the physical. There is not one law for the physical and another for the spirit, but one law for both.

Vibrations increase in geometrical progression, and it is a well known fact that there are long skips in the scale where mortal ear hears and eye perceives, for motion becomes so rapid that it is lost to sight and sound. Watch the spokes of a locomotive wheel as the speed increases, they appear first blurred, then continuous. As the speed still increases they pass from our vision, as completely as spirit-form does. Both are governed by the same law. We do not see the spirit-forms of men or animals simply because of their vibratory condition; that is to say, the average mortal does not; but there are some men and women who can catch sounds from the spirit world and others who can see spirit-forms; that is, they are psychic; they can see things and hear sounds that the average mortal cannot. This is termed "clairvoyance," and "clairaudience." Then again there are two forms of each one, the outward and the inward: (a) The outward form is where the psychic sees the form of a person, thing or object, or hears sound produced in the ear; this is a question of being attuned to higher than ordinary vibrations; (b) the inward form is where a spirit is able to impress or to make the image directly upon the spirit-brain of the person, or to impress thoughts on the subconscious mind. This latter form is generally called impression or inspiration, but this too, is only a question of vibration. A psychic is also known as, and in fact is, a "sensitive," who is able, to an extraordinary degree, to catch sights and sounds that the average individual cannot.

There are birds whose homes are among the crags and high altitudes of the Andes, whose song mortal ear has never heard; yet many men have seen their bills open and close with lightning rapidity and their throats pulsate, but the song is pitched so high that it fails to vibrate on mortal ear.

Again one said:

"All life is the expression of the overmastering energy of atoms. Vibratory action in the physical world is the ceaseless action and reaction of one force upon another—one undulating wave on another undulating wave. There is never an instant when this action ceases. It is at once the process of elimination, rejection, propulsion, discord and harmony. Nature is apparently relentless. The sweeping storm, the force of the fire and tornado, destroy alike the gnarled oak and the perfectly formed landscape. Mortals with limited physical vision look with horror upon the devastation wrought, but we who have clearer vision see that this is only nature's mode of house cleaning. Out of the chaos, the great law of vibration produces harmony. A universal peace and calmness follow the ravages of the destructive elements. Why should this be so? Because all atoms have been brought together, governed by this law, then as quickly separated ; and, after having been hurled apart and crashing here and there, the similar particles fall into harmony once more."

"*I* am fully conscious that any other statement of this law; of vibration must, of necessity, be closely related to the theories of creation. It must fulfil a triple purpose; it must be not only cause and effect but the strange, indefinable, intermediate step that is the growth, as it were, of the real into the unreal. This triple purpose is revealed in the ceaseless action of the positive and negative qualities of every atom. In its power of repulsion and attraction, in its differences and similarities, this law governs the slowly-dissolving elements of every period of the earth's formation from nothingness, nameless ether, into harmony of activity; from this activity into form; from form to organized being; from organized being into other forms of being which again dissolve, and again form, completing a circle back again into nameless nothingness, ether, and the essence of force. When the vibrations grow gradually less, the form begins to be manifested and we have the atom, the molecule, the electric spark, the physical expression of life.

"The freed spirit comprehends the laws of vibratory physical action. To know is to be outside of: hence, not until we have become disembodied, do we truly know. As disembodied spirits we cannot *experience*. That belongs to earth-life alone; it is an illusive teacher. Not until we cease experiencing, can we grasp the law that governs. The subconscious mind, governed by this law, grasps it, adds to it, repels and attracts, and moulds itself over and over until, finally, you of earth-life, get a little appreciation of it."

This is a new theory in the philosophy of man. But towards its proper comprehension the thought of the twentieth century will be directed; and, with the mastery of the elementary principles will come greater appreciation of the future condition of man, in the life beyond the physical.

XII. Matter

ALL matter is composed of molecules, atoms and electrons. A molecule is made up of several atoms. For instance, a molecule of water is composed of three atoms, two of hydrogen and one of oxygen. The atoms are very small, about one hundred thousandth of an inch in size, and yet sufficient in number to make up the mass of all the planets composing the solar systems of the universe. These small particles possess a force so wonderful that it is utterly impossible for man to follow and examine them, for the reason that they are constantly changing in their rapid passage. They pass through the ether with wave-like undulatory motion, and, like human beings, have their likes and dislikes. When they find their affinity, we have what is known as cohesion, for every particle of matter has an attraction for other particles. These atoms have a force and a heat that all the furnaces of earth could not produce. Under certain conditions, however, there may be a loss of heat, and, if it were possible, in the laboratories of earth to expel heat entirely from the atoms composing matter, it would become practically lifeless and inert. This, however, is impossible; therefore, while they possess heat and force, they may be solid, liquid and gaseous, in which latter condition they may be said to bump against each other, rebound and move freely through ether which not only joins with the atmosphere surrounding this planet, but connects far distant worlds; and this ether, this subtle air, around and about us, permeates all substances.

In the wondrous atoms, with their likes and dislikes, attracting other atoms through the ether and in continual action, we have *force, motion* and *electrified heat.*

Atoms are split up and again subdivided, and those smaller particles are called electrons ; that is, they are electrified. In other words, they carry electrified points, not the electricity that we behold in the lightning flash or in magnet and coil, but a small subtle electricity which mortal man does not yet comprehend. Electrons, then, are really the electrified points of the sub-divided atom, the polarized particles, not one of which could be spared out of the universe. A single atom cannot be lost, it has its place, its power and its task to do.

The world of matter is a world of change. Molecules changing, atoms changing, electrons changing, but the subtle spirit which permeates them is never lost. Each possesses a spark of life-force from the great ocean of Infinity which is immortal.

When we speak, ordinarily, of matter, we refer to sensible substances which offer resistance to the touch and to muscular effort, and which is indestructible an(d eternal, which reacts against external force, is permanent and preserves its identity under all changes. Again, matter is everything that possesses the properties of *gravity* and *attraction*.

While I am not able to state it as a fact, I am of the opinion, reasoning by deduction, that the laws of gravitation act only upon matter the vibration of which is so slow that it is physical; that when the vibration is increased to what we know as spirit or mind, the law of gravitation no longer acts upon it; then the law of attraction is the dominating force. The force of gravitation is in direct lines only; the lines of attraction reach in all directions. Gravitation then, acts upon the physical body only; attraction, upon the mental state. And after separation from the body, the spirit, freed from physical substance, is free from the control and influence of the laws of gravitation, for which reason spirit people move freely and at will within the boundaries of their sphere.

There is not in the physical universe, as far as known, a substance that is actually solid. A cubic inch of the hardest steel differs from a cubic inch of air only in the arrangement and position of its atoms and molecules. It is all a question of density and vibration. Could a magnifying glass be made powerful enough, what is known as solid matter would appear like dust floating in the sun's rays, for nothing is ever actually still. Nature abhors stagnation as it does a vacuum. All in the universe is matter, whether physical or spiritual, composed of atoms and molecules attracted and associated in varying and different degrees of density and therefore of vibration. All substance is, in fact, matter, whether it be visible or invisible, whether it be sensible to touch or elusive. In accordance with this theory of advanced science, all matter is progressing into modes of motion, dissolving into activity, and so shading off into that great reality that is all energy and life.

Can there be energy without substance; does not everything that has expression necessitate substance? The idea that spirit-people exist but are unsubstantial is illogical and preposterous. The gases which compose water, taken separately, are as much substance as when united. The spirit-body is as much substance as a physical body. Why should it be considered impossible for mother nature to clothe spirits with substance so that, when separated from flesh, both should continue to exist as absolutely as when joined together? When we pass into the spirit-life, we have the same features, the same general contour, the same proportions, and we carry that normal condition wherever we go. Our shape, size, features and contour are determined by the spiritual atoms forming our spiritual personality, and this continues through all spheres. Thus our identity, once established, exists in continuity with life,—remaining always the same, being always composed of the same personal atoms.

All that exists in positive condition is matter; intelligent forces permeate all material things, and are made manifest in motion. Motion is moving matter. Matter, in a very high state of vibratory action, may be, and frequently is, classed as immaterial; but, in reality, there is no immaterial thing; an absolutely immaterial thing would be absolutely nothing—so-called immaterial things are conditions of matter in a very great degree of sublimation. We cannot conceive of anything made out of nothing.

Electricity and magnetism are highly sublimated conditions of matter; one step further finds us in the world of Spirit, which is a still greater degree of material sublimation. The electro-magnetic may be so nearly related to the condition of spiritual sublimation as to be the connecting link between mind, or spirit, and matter; but we are not, as yet, able to grasp the condition of magnetic, electric, and spiritual vibration to any extent. Investigation causes growth step by step, until, by and by, we may understand the force of electro-magnetism.

Matter disappears from our vision, but reappears to our senses. This thing called matter, which, in one state or another, is perfectly opaque, and will not permit a ray of light to pass through it, will in another form, which is spirit, become perfectly transparent. The cause of this wonderful change is beyond our comprehension. Science may say it is due to some attraction in the position or arrangement of atoms or molecules; but atoms or molecules, however confident the "scientists" may be of their existence and of the laws that govern their attraction and repulsion, are beyond the reach of our physical senses.

Substances dissolved in water or burned in the air, are not annihilated, for, by certain well known means, they can be recalled and restored to sight, some in exactly the same state as before they became invisible, others in some other state or condition. Matter is indestructible; if there is matter, there must be spirit, for matter is only the substance that spirit uses for physical expression. Spirit, whether it finds physical expression or whether it exists apart from gross matter, as we use that term, is of primary importance and is the first subject for consideration, while the garment which makes life visible is only of secondary importance. One law, as we have shown, governs all conditions in the physical as well as in the spirit planes; and whenever we find lifeforces, they are clothed with either physical or spiritual material, which is matter in different states of vibrations. So that the *individual life,* at dissolution, undergoes a change of vibration, like water changed into vapor; it is the same life still having form, feature, and expression, just as before, but changed in its vibratory action, the atoms pulsate at a higher rate so that they are no longer visible to us. Though matter still, they pass from our sight like steam dissolved in air.

Mind is matter, and day by day, and minute by minute, as it crystalizes, it takes definite form and shape; and its creations are clothed with substance. Some are given physical expression in works of art, inventions, books, and buildings; but the great majority find expression in what we term spirit-matter, of which man comes to a full appreciation only as he passes into that sphere of usefulness. Matter, in this physical world, is changed and fashioned by hands or by machinery made by hands, so low is its vibratory condition; but, as we ascend in the scale of life, thought becomes such a wonderful force that it can fashion, model and mould substances that vibrate in similar waves into actual forms of its own creations. In this way, the environment that a spirit finds after dissolution is found to be one that he has, perhaps unknown to himself, been creating by his acts and by his thought from day to day.

Thought is the one great thing in the universe. Formed and fashioned in the human brain, it is projected into the ether, that permeates all things and all space, by laws we are not yet able to comprehend. It takes form and shape and awaits there

our coming. The homes which spirit-people have, and the condition in and about them, their very location, depend on the life-work and thought action of the individual. Everything is governed by law; nothing happens by chance; cause and effect are as potent in the spirit plane as in the earth plane. These facts must be borne in mind: All is matter, here and hereafter; spirit-people have bodies; their identity never changes; they have homes; they are real; they are people; and they live after what we call death.

On this subject, I am told:

"Spirit is ethereal matter—matter whose home is in ether, which is higher in vibration than the atmosphere in which it formerly existed. Each change into another sphere is a higher, more vitalizing vibration, until the emancipated spirit reaches a sphere of most intense vibration, which holds the power of life. Then it can impregnate matter in a lower material condition, and give it an atom of spirit to develop. The reason that man is continually growing in spiritual thought, is because as this force, this life-giving force, increases, it becomes stronger, and man is being equipped for the development of his spiritual being.

"Matter includes all things that have continued life,— and we know that nothing can die. Ether is the atmosphere of spirit-people. From each man in his natural condition emanates spiritual ether. It is because of this atmosphere that we are able to come close to him, and thereby reach his subconscious mind."

Spirit-material is nothing more than earthly matter raised to a higher degree of activity; while spirit-force is pure force. The physical world is a counterpart of the spirit world, but the latter is the reality.

There are more than five avenues of knowledge. There is much about matter that we do not know. It is possible to pass matter through matter. Recall the flowers heretofore mentioned, brought from a distance, passed through the walls of the room in which we were, and reconstructed. How was it done? Spirit chemists know how to use this subtle electric power to reduce the atoms that are solid, to a gaseous state. Oxygen at low temperature and under pressure, can be transformed into a solid; it can also be reduced to a liquid and changed into ether. Physical substance, under such treatment, becomes gaseous and etheric, and may, by a similar process, be restored to its normal conditions. In this manner the flowers were de-materialized and again materialized. The process was simply a chemical change.

Savages rubbing sticks to produce fire, looked upon the traveler with suspicion and fear; but when they saw him produce fire with a match, their souls were filled with wonder. Spirit-people look with sorrow upon the people of this generation, for the great majority, in their simplicity, are still rubbing sticks to obtain light, though the sun shines in the heavens.

XIII. Limitations Of Science

THERE are many things that science does not know, and will never discover, unless it abandons methods which limit and narrow its field of operation. It has confined itself to the prescribed task of investigating gross matter, until even that has eluded its grasp in the form of simple force, and left it empty-handed. It has peered into the heavens with its telescopes and looked a little farther into matter with its microscopes; but it has come no nearer to the nature of things than it was in the beginning.

When chemistry put the key of the physical universe into its hands, it was enough to devote a century to the dazzling picture it revealed,—a century of concentrated and universal gaze at the world, out of whose dust our material bodies are made, and in which life-forces find visible expression; but, having sat so long before the elementary flames and having seen matter reduced to gas and force, and there stop, the world has become impatient at its inability to answer further questions. While we have been shown the component parts of our physical bodies, and how our actions are linked to the invariable energy of the universe, science has not explained us ourselves, nor analyzed us in its retort, nor measured us by the law of continuity.

Chemistry has led to biology, this in turn to psychology, and this to sociology, history and religion; and the patient world has, at last, growing dissatisfied, asked science to analyze consciousness, mind, thought and love; but science cannot meet those demands ; it has pushed its researches until it has reached confines beyond which it cannot go, though it does see forces which it cannot explain. Science starts with matter in its homogeneous state of diffusion, that is, at so-called rest and without action, either externally so, or as the result of exhausted force. Now, we ask whence comes this force? Science has no answer except that which is involved in the vague phrase "unknowable cause," which is a contradiction of terms, since a cause with a visible result is, to that extent, known. The law of gravitation goes before its action. What of the origin of the law that acts on matter? Why does it begin to act on matter while at rest? Again, how do we pass from the functional action of the brain to consciousness? The scientists claim that the chasm is impassible. What, then, will they do with the fact and phenomena of consciousness? Again, what right has science, knowing nothing of the origin of force, and, therefore, understanding nothing of its nature, to limit its action and potentiality to the "functional" play of organism? Again, they test and measure matter by mind, but if matter be tested and measured by mind, it is, as it were, one clod or crystal analyzing another. It is like getting into the scales with the thing to be weighed.

Metaphysics is an entirely new philosophy, dealing with energy and life-forces, separate and apart from that material which the physical world terms matter, governed by entirely different laws and using new methods in its demonstrations.

It is greatly to be regretted that scientists, who have made such wonderful progress in knowledge of the material world, stand so much in awe of each other that very few of them have had the courage to depart from their antiquated system of investigation. In the few instances where great minds have dared to investigate questions transcending physical science, they have been subjected to the ridicule and derision of the great majority of their fellows, who have not had the courage to venture beyond old, accepted theories. To those who have had the courage of their convictions, and the breadth of mind to associate this new philosophy with their own personalities, men like Sir Oliver Lodge, for example, great credit is due; but physicists, as a class, have no right to come into this new field, for which they are so unqualified. Neither have they any right to criticize methods and means which they do not understand; nor have they any right to say: "If there are laws that govern life-force apart from gross material, they must be discovered by us." Let them confine their efforts to their own field of matter and its development, and leave the study of life-forces to others who labor in new ways and who have to grapple with higher problems than those of physics.

We, of the newer philosophy, demonstrate the limitations of science when we ask of it: "What is the relation of mind to the senses?" The observing senses are before the thinking mind. We might also ask: "What is the nature of this thing that you call matter, which you think you can feel and see? But *how* do you see it, and how do you feel it? You do not know."

We of the newer school, having, at least, nothing to unlearn, stand in no fear of the criticism of any man or class of men. Having discovered new and original methods by which we comprehend something of the economy of natural laws and coming, as we have, into direct communication with people in the after-life with whom we discuss such problems; having been told something of these heretofore unanswerable questions —something of force, energy, mind, soul, spirit and its relation to matter, by men who have become truly great, we labor to increase the knowledge of mankind, and to gain a better appreciation of our place in nature and of our relation to her.

The field is so vast, the questions are so great, the opportunities so limited, and the subject is so new, that we can at most obtain only a little knowledge, and enunciate only a few of the primary laws that govern all things animate and inanimate.

There are sounds that our ears have never heard; there is light that our physical eyes can never see; there is an invisible world filled with people that few here ever imagined. And yet, discoveries are made from year to year of these invisible people and inaudible things, through the patient labors of earnest workers. Step by step, we grasp and comprehend these laws, each one based on those that go before. Crooke's tubes have been in use since 1878, and Roentgen's rays were in existence for nearly twenty years before their presence was even suspected. Just as the great invisible world was unknown, and just as those rays remained so long undiscovered, so even now there exist in the universe spirit-people, and other rays, other vibrations, of which, as yet, we have little cognizance. The seemingly trivial observations made by one worker, lead to useful observations by another, and so progress makes its way, creeping from point to point; and so, year by year, the sum-total of our knowledge increases, and our ignorance is rolled further and further back. Where there is darkness, there will be light; and where there was ignorance, there must come knowledge. Such is the law of mental evolution.

Science, as such, deals only with gases, fluids and solids; with length, breadth, and thickness. In such a domain, and amongst such phenomena, no hint, even, of future existence can be found; and science only says: "I find no report of it?"

In accounting for all things, shall we be limited to matter and force? Science says: "Yes, because matter and force are all we know or can know." Another school says: "Matter and force account for all things; thought, will and consciousness." Another admits the existence of something else, but claims it to be "unknowable."

All that physical science is able to discern is matter in its lower conditions. The spirit world, as well as the physical, is a field of legitimate inquiry. The barriers that craft and superstition have erected are being swept away; the laws that govern the process of death are as well defined as those that govern the process of life. They are purely chemical and equally absolute and irrevocable.

To the masses, spirit-life is a mystery; death a hopeless problem; while the world of the invisible, just another community all around us, cannot be comprehended by the average mortal mind.

We have our limitations. Our work, while not of, must center largely about, the physical, as the mind of mortal man cannot get far beyond the evidence that pertains to the physical senses. The revelations from the other world are only just begun, yet the effect upon the human mind is already marvelous. The power of the new school to accomplish great results is limited only by the perceptive capacity of the brain. The best way for each one is to pursue his own investigations, to make his own demonstrations, until the force of the facts breaks upon the inner consciousness. We are entering a great region of undiscovered knowledge which yet remains to be explored by those who search for truth. He who enters this field of intellectual labor, needs no preconceived beliefs, but a mind, like a sensitive plate, on which facts may be impressed.

Through the avenue of metaphysics we have seen that we may climb to many higher planes of thought. Physical science cannot accept that which it cannot define. The physicist must have a label on everything, and assumes that what is incomprehensible to him, must, necessarily, be false! He says that he admits the existence of a soul, and then proceeds to tear the idea into shreds, leaving the mind of a man of average education in a state of complete chaos. Opposed to this narrow and unsatisfactory method, which physical science has adopted in dealing with spiritual entities, the viewpoint of metaphysics is distinctly vital; in other words, it maintains that the physicist, or the chemist, is unable to explain the principle of life without the aid of higher knowledge. And this fact alone shows the necessity for a philosophy of metaphysics.

XIV. The Attitude Of Science

WE are apt, with our physical environment, to stand in awe of so-called "Men of Science," and expect that all progress, spiritual as well as material, will come through them.

I have never agreed with the methods adopted by them to prove the continuity of life. Many attempt to build their structures by tearing down; to establish a fact by a process of elimination; they try to prove a thing is so, by proving it is not so. This method, I am led to believe, is erroneous in dealing with forces beyond the physical plane.

The judgment of spirit-people, with their greater knowledge and experience, is interesting. One now in spirit-life, who has advanced far, made this startling statement which I have hesitated to publish:

"All proper respect is due and payable to the man of learning. But when learning, be it the result of book-study, of experimental investigation, or of knowledge imparted from one to another, has the effect of making men self-important, so that they adopt such an attitude towards others as to imply that all wisdom and knowledge repose solely and entirely in themselves, then I say that the so-called men of learning only make themselves ridiculous, and that the institutions which produce savants of this type are defective, and antagonistic to real intellectual progress.

"No one has a greater feeling of respect and admiration than I have for men who have, by constant and patient effort, sought to unravel and explain those great laws of the universe, the proper understanding of which tends to help and to advance their fellow-men. We all salute the man who does things; but we also feel contempt for that egotistic group of socialists, to be found in every country, who are always seeking to surround the laws of the universe with a hidden meaning, and to throw a halo around themselves and the cult they seek to organize, by erecting an artificial superstructure of baseless theory upon the facts already explained by the earnest worker, who has by toil and study revealed some hitherto unknown law. The genuine scholar is a plain man of simple ways, somewhat reserved in his expressions and criticisms, because what he knows makes him diffident about speaking in an adverse manner of new propositions which he has not investigated. But the self-satisfied man, who, because of the fact that he, by some chance, has become enrolled among the members of a cult, pretends to know everything and dares to doubt everything, while in reality too shallow for thorough knowledge, is often found among so-called scientists.

"Are there not notes in the scale too high in their vibration for mortal ear? Are there not colors belonging to the rays of the spectrum, too rapid in their vibration to be detected by the mortal eye? Yes, of course. Why 'of course?' Because science has proved it! Nonsense! Let us ask ourselves, What is science? I will tell you what science is. It is the result of the determining of the why, and the wherefore, of a few of nature's laws that existed for ages before this word science was invented. Poor mortal man! His opportunities for advancement have been one long succession of trials. First he was obliged to overcome his visible enemies and the fear of the wilderness; then, when he had gained a little confidence, a combination of men arose and ensnared him by fear of the so-called supernatural; and then, when he dared to tell that set of men, 'Begone' so that he might think alone; behold! another set of men arose, who told him that he could think only as they should decide.

"Pray, tell me, what has any man of science, no matter how arrogant his claims may be, accomplished to entitle him to say that he holds the key to all knowledge? For each discoverer of a new scientific principle by which the world is benefited, there are a hundred, who, if they had been guided by 'science' only, would have remained all their lives in intellectual stagnation, but who have, with spirit-assistance, been able to enlarge the boundaries of human knowledge by a proper application of nature's laws. If the word 'science' be confined to knowledge of the laws of the physical world merely, it covers only a small field. The laws of spirit are far more important than the laws of our bodily structure.

Man's spiritual future is a grander field of inquiry than the principles of mechanics."

Another said:

"To treat the subject of psychic phenomena by analysis, as you would treat matter, is not within the province of mortals. The soul is the spirit, and can be apprehended by mortals only by the operation of a thinking mind. 'Whence comest thou?' 'Whither goest thou?' These are the two great questions for all, and all must some day have the power to answer them. Would not a comprehensive knowledge of these questions be of inestimable benefit to you in your earth-life? Many a great and grievous error might have been avoided, and many who suffer might have been made happy, had it been universally realized that the earth-life is but a preparatory school for a future condition, where progress or retardment of progress is the result of one's own actions.

"It is well that mortals should live the earth-life in accordance with the laws of nature, and not spend too much time in speculative thought as to the why and wherefore of his being; but good being the desire of all, or the necessary condition of all for advancement, a true knowledge of the future state of the spirit is necessary that errors of life may not occur, through your own unguided actions.

"A knowledge of the continued life after passing from earth, cannot be determined by weighing, measuring, or comparing, as is done with material things; but by an acceptance of truth, manifested by the power of mind. There having been no beginning, there will be no ending of nature or of natural laws. Is it then to be said that mortal man is to be the sole exception in this eternal order of things? As you are, so shall you be. Your path lies onward; death, as you term it, being but a single step, an unimportant change in the journey. Everything moves forward, nothing backward. The ending of mortal existence is but the first change to usefulness. You must not consider that the law that applies to constant improvement, does not apply to the lowest as well as to the highest in life.

"The principle that leads some men of science to hold that the only true laws are those provable by his deepest investigation and research, is a great error. After the limit of investigation has been reached, there are many more questions to be answered that are as yet unanswerable; this being so, you must seek for the answers by a process of philosophic reasoning.

"Great minds require proof of small things, and this is right; but it does not require that great truths should be placed before great minds. Many minds of more simple attainment, grasp great truths much more easily than do minds which possess the quality of greatness."

Another, who while in this life was a well known preacher, says:

"I should like to add my mite to your epistle to the 'scientists' and to tell them that the life for which they try to find a scientific, materialistic reason, is as wonderful and as eternal as the universe; they cannot end it by death, any more than they can produce it by artificial means. Life comes from the great force of a mighty blending of souls which permeates all things and all space; life enters in, and is taken up by the material atoms, when nature's law, which governs all things, deem the conditions in a productive state. The amount of this great force, which is retained by the being as it develops, depends largely upon the condition of the soil in which it is planted.

"All the talking, thinking and surmising, of all the minds in the world, cannot bring about the birth of a soul; and the great power that can generate a soul may be trusted to look after it justly and carefully after death. That death is the end, is a belief that a well balanced mind cannot accept. Life would be but a futile thing, and all effort useless, if the future did not stretch before us endless and unlimited in its possibilities. Believe me, the justice that meets the naked soul, on the threshold of its spirit-life, is terrible in its completeness! If the understanding of this truth could only reach people during earth-life, they would escape much sorrow,—sorrow intensified to a degree greater than earth-dwellers can conceive."

Great was my gratification to receive the following statement, from a man well known on earth, which I here give word for word:

"Tell your fellow-workers for me that I was working on a material plane all the years of my earth-life; that since I passed out, I have found that the material is but a fleeting thing in the real existence of the soul; that the nearer a man lets himself come to the spiritual, so as to accept suggestion and help from a higher source than the material, the nearer he will come to an understanding of life in its true sense. All these theories about another sense are ridiculous and were begotten in the brains of clever men, who were unable to give up their own petty ideas. They wanted to create, to make the laws that govern the universe; but I tell you that those laws have already been made,—they are fixed and unalterable, and the sooner the mass of mankind realizes this, and comes to a true and definite conception of the simplicity and justice of those laws, the sooner will they live lives fitted to carry them up the next step of progress. They must accept life and its governing forces as they are, at some period; therefore, the sooner the better. I am anxious to be the means of bringing light to some brilliant minds. But they must learn to accept the truth, to put themselves aside, and to realize that as it was in the beginning, it is now, and ever shall be. I am profoundly impressed with this fact: either men of science must grasp these higher laws, or let this new thought fall into other hands."

I do not mean, by quoting from the speech of spirit-people, to attempt to belittle, if that were possible, the achievement of modern scientific men, for they have done a great deal for material progress. But I do say that they have not done everything; for many great discoveries of nature's hidden laws have come from unknown and unclassed sensitive brains subject to spirit suggestion.

The "scientists," as a class, are materialistic and know little of any forces outside of matter in its lower manifestations. But these men have made psychics respectable, and the world will ever remain indebted to them, for, by their personality, they have dignified research.

Men like Alfred Russell Wallace, Sir William Crooke, Sir Oliver Lodge, Camille Flammarion, Dr. Charles Richet and others have had sufficient greatness of mind to break through the limited bonds of physical science, and to tell the world that there are laws in matter, and beyond matter, of which they have evidence, and that life continues beyond what is known as dissolution.

This also has been said to me:

"If men of science, with all their knowledge and eager quest for the how and wherefore of all things, would only consent to learn a little of something beyond their actual touch! I know some do not deny the existence of life after death, but they spend all their time and effort in proving, to their own satisfaction, whether a few insignificant spirits really are whom they claim to be, instead of making their investigation dignified and useful by learning something of that future life, and the best way of getting ready to enter it."

The present attitude of science is of no importance except as in so far as it presumes wholly to preempt this field of research, which is the domain of the individual. We can come as near to the heart of nature, and can understand the simple laws of life that find no physical expression, as they can who formed the hypothesis of the molecule and measure the stars. We have eyes, and we see what nature has created; and ears upon whose drums fall all the wealth of sound. We taste the fruits and smell the perfume of all that grows, and with our hands fashion and build what the brain conceives. The man of science has no other senses, and can do no more.

I do honor those earnest men who have done so much for the material progress of the world. Their mastery of the physical side of nature has challenged the admiration of all, and the future, in so far as it relates to such matters, is largely in their keeping; but, in this field of psychic research, they are as yet trying to prove an axiom. I do question the methods adopted by them. The Master Mind has not reserved to any class the exclusive privilege of discovery. The University of Nature is the greatest institution in the world; its doors are thrown open to all who seek to know her ways, to which no coterie hold the key. Her vast treasure-house is full, and she gives with a prodigal hand. All who would know her wondrous laws, and thereby enrich themselves, must, by a process of elimination, free their minds, and, like children, approach the throne of knowledge. They may say these facts are not accepted by science, that I cannot demonstrate them by their man-made rules, that they are not evidential. This may all be true according to their understanding I but I answer: many facts in nature are provable by laws in common use by those who have studied metaphysics, and it is the great desire of individuals in the great beyond that men of science adopt those laws, applicable only to matter in the higher conditions of vibration and discard in this field of investigation those laws that only apply to matter so slow in vibration that it is physical. If this be done they will enrich the spirit as they have enriched the material world.

XV. Evolution

LITTLE is known of that constant force known as evolution, or of the great laws that govern the process of advancement. I have eagerly sought information on this subject, have discussed it with many men in the next sphere beyond and have been told, among other things:

"A most encouraging indication of the progress of the present age is the fact that a few great thinkers and demonstrators of nature's laws have been able to grasp conditions beyond the physical, and are giving such information to mortals, who, because of their environment and duties, have not been able to solve for themselves these great problems.

"You ask me to say something concerning evolution, meaning that gradual, and yet positive, change in the world's condition that has finally resulted in *thinking mankind*. So be it. Then is not what I have just said a most wonderful and beautiful illustration of the progressive realization of the Master's great purpose—the gradual, yet positive, improvement of matter *until an observant and grateful mortal is the final result?*

"God, as you use the word, is the All. That is apparent to every thinking brain. Being, then, that All, God cannot be a personality; every bit of matter is a part and parcel of that All; every force in nature is an expression of the presence of that All; and every thinking brain is a more or less perfect functional part of that All.

"To a sane and appreciative, active brain, free alike from arrogance and illusion, the proposition that mortal man is made in the perfect image of his Master, God, is the extreme of egotistical blasphemy. Far better is the expression of your countryman, Robert G. Ingersoll, that "Man has made God in his image." That part of mortal man that is in any degree like his Master is his thinking brain; otherwise, man is but an expression, in his form and physical functions, of that process of evolution spoken of as environment. All that is great in man is mind, and this greatness increases as he rises to the level of the ideal, the Master-Mind.

"In a previous discussion, I mentioned the fact that we spirit-people do not always agree on many subjects of which we have no actual proof or convincing evidence, and so as regards the early stages of earth and the subsequent changes up to the existence of man, many among us differ; but I am safe in saying that the best informed hold that there has been a constant refining process of earth-matter since the cooling of the evidently original vaporous particles that gradually, by loss of heat, become solidified into rock and water; and that as the chaotic condition gradually assumed a proper separation upon cooling and solidifying, the process of refining gross matter began, and by the action of element upon element, of substance upon substance, the erosion of the primitive rock occurred, with the result of eliminating the fine from the gross; and, by the action of water in causing sedimentary deposits and the raising or lowering of the sedimentary or refined rock, and the consequent re-refining process, chemical action was allowed to come into play, resulting in a continuation of the process whereby gross matter is refined. Necessarily, as the cooling mass must have constantly given off heat, and also absorbed a certain amount of heat by chemical action, there came a period when the earth's crust could support the first life, vegetation. This vegetable life itself is but the chemical product of certain parts of refined matter, resulting from the gradual solidifying of the gaseous vapors fixed in space by the action of some of the planets undergoing a change.

"As regards the earth's actual beginning, there is no authentic knowledge among spirit-people. A theory based upon sound premises may be regarded as a general statement of the truth. From a knowledge of existing conditions, comparative reasoning can, and does, draw correct deductions, and so men of scientific attainments have, by study and investigations, demonstrated much that is not only evidence, but that may be said to be actually demonstrated.

"Among the best informed of the spirit-people the growth of a new planet results from the fixing in space, by the existing stellar system,—owing to that great principle of nature known as the law of gravitation, of some mass of matter revolving wildly through the universe, and the placing of it in a position of harmony with other masses of matter or planets. So must the earth have been caught when in its state of motion and vaporous matter, conditioned by its flight through space, not by any friction of the particles of its mass against the so-called ether, but because of the unusual disturbance of the particles of the mass among themselves; and also, because of the latent heat imparted to the runaway mass of matter that may be considered the nucleus of your planet. When finally caught and held in its place of rest, by that great principle of gravity, as in its mad career it came into the lines of force existing from other planetary bodies, by gradual degrees, its speed was steadied and, slowly but surely, it fell into that correct and dignified motion that is consistent with the laws governing planets, and it became one of the necessary keystones in the constellations of which it must have been elected a member. And so a new planet was born. Man has since called it earth. All the essentials of the present conditions existed at the very beginning of the earth's creation, have ever been, and are now, stored away in the mass of fugitive matter.

"Evolution is but the action of that great power called by mortal man, God, but which really is the process of refinement and purification of gross matter until the resultant product *is living thinking mortal man,* and then the intellectual man. The next step in that ever-changing, ever-progressing evolution, is the endowment of that physical, intellectual man, with what we call spirit.

"As each and every particle of matter depends upon some other particle of matter to allow of that progressive refinement spoken of, so is it throughout the entire chain, and spirit-people are as necessary to physical people as the gas exhaled from the lungs of living animalism is for the growth of vegetation, or as the refined chemical vegetable combinations are to animal life."

The origin of life has been, and ever will be, a great mystery, until such time as we shall, by progression out of the body, come to a greater understanding of life force. We all know something of the process by which all planetary life, both animal and vegetable, is started; but the principal process of inoculation of matter with life-forces, is practically unknown, though we do know that it is governed by law. In the discussion of this great problem of the origin of life, we must take matter into consideration in its different vibratory conditions, from the generic rock to the Universal Mind.

As I have said before, when life, in its evolution, progresses so that it has *power of thought* and constructive reasoning, it has reached a stage of individualism that can never be lost. This power of thought and constructive reasoning, then, is the line of demarcation which determines whether the particular life force is to continue and hold individuality beyond the physical, or pass into some other form of gross matter. There is no matter in the universe which does not possess atomic energy, and, therefore, lifeforce. When matter is brought to the proper state of vibration by physical action, and sufficiently refined; when, in other words, according to a natural law, temperature is increased and matter is rendered receptive because of its activity, an atom of Universal Good, of life-force, inoculates, enters into it, and it becomes clothed, and after the required period of gestation and growth, there is a physical birth.

It is, in reality, matter acting on matter; refined matter, or spirit, clothing itself with grosser material, thus obtaining physical expression and individuality. The atom of Good that finds individual expression in every birth is from the great ocean of Infinite Mind or Universal Good. Prior to conception, it was not individual; but from that moment it commences its journey back to the sphere of Exaltation, the highest mental state of which we can have any knowledge.

This life-force that finds expression in mankind, or in the animal or vegetable kingdom, is all from the same source; but just what it develops into depends upon the character of the matter with which it is clothed, and its evolution, to a large extent, depends upon subsequent environment.

Species have always been, and will always be, distinct in character. You cannot make a radical change except to improve it. Nature has created all species for distinct purposes; nothing lives that has not a place and a purpose. Whether man understands, appreciates, and comprehends this fact or not, it is true. It would be the changing of a natural law to change species.

Evolution, then, starts on the earth plane with an atom of Universal Good, clothed and individualized in this sphere of development and of preparation for the real life, which only commences with physical dissolution. Evolution is forward, not backward. The atom of life-force, which finds physical expression here, prompted, urged, and taught by spirit-intelligences as well as by parental suggestion, develops; and, at some time very early in life, comes to use reason; wants to know; thinks; looks upon the wonders of earth and sky and marvels. That life, so started upon its journey, growing to maturity, and passing to greater opportunity, by laws as irresistible as force, goes on and on, with but one opportunity for physical development, while he, a mortal being, journeys upon this globe. There is no coming back to live this life over again; no reincarnation; but everlasting and continued progress and development. Evolution springs from the desire to know, to see, to feel, to understand and to grasp all natural laws; and, as the individual grows, becomes more refined, and increases the ratio of his thought vibration, he reaches higher planes in the progress of his earth development.

Evolution is not confined to life-force, but matter, as we use that term, develops in a corresponding degree. Of this we have material evidence.

There are three perceptible stages in the evolution of form: (a) Increase in the mass; (b) decrease in the stability of the molecules; (c) increase in the activity of the substances. The evolution of each material form comes by adding atom to atom in their dimensions, making distinct the unity of composition existing between the mental states, all pulsating at a higher and higher rate. This is positive evidence of evolution.

"Evolution means progress, higher development. Each vibratory atom must go through each stage of vibration before it can be fitted for the fullest perfection. The story of evolution may be seen in the grain of wheat. It is planted and then develops through each successive stage until it becomes nourishment for man, and thence its development is a part of a souls progress; and eventually it becomes a part of the life-force, and generates life-force into another grain of wheat, and each new grain that reaches the life-force enriches it and makes more powerful that force, so that, while it completes a perfect circle, yet it is always growing greater and more perfect. Thus evolution is constantly repeating itself on a larger scale each time."

Wherever there is life-force there must be thought. There is intelligent action embodied in every seed that has a living germ. The acorn has sense enough to send its roots into the earth, its trunk and branches into the air, and to choose for food for root and branch, such elements as will make the oak tree, and to reject such elements as would be proper only for the pine. All grass has the same kind of intelligence in choosing food, and the power of choice must involve the power of thought. All the laws of nature, being universal in their application, apply to all life alike; what is true of the grain of wheat is true of man. The evolution of one is similar to that of the other, and is destined to increase the life-force of the universe. Knowledge is a pyramid with its base buried in the organic, towering higher and higher as it increases; and crowning the whole, embodying all of nature's handiwork, is the master-builder, man. What could be grander, more noble and beautiful, than the human mind at work under the guidance and suggestion of spirit-people, who have progressed beyond the comprehension of earth conceptions?

Evolution began with the primeval, nebulous mass, in which was held, potentially, all future worlds. Under evolutionary laws the amorphous cloud broke up, condensed, took definite shape and, in time, assumed a gradually increasing complexity. Finally, there emerged the cooled and finished earth, highly differentiated; and there was given us the breeding ground for the inception of life and for the organization of the elements into the first relation of sentient form. What has passed in history many know, but what evolution finally leads to in its progression, mortal man will never know. That is the province of spirit-people.

When they have passed out of the earth conditions, because of evolutionary laws, spirit-people have beautiful flowers, far away hills, majestic mountains, leaping brooks, blossoming orchards, musical birds, the storm and lightning flash, the disturbed ocean, the clearing sky and the setting sun with tints of many colors. All that we have is but an imitation of the *reality* which belongs to their sphere only. Of course, what they have differs from what we have because of a higher and more rapid vibration, but the effect is similar.

The tendency of all life, wherever found or however clothed, is to perfect, improve, increase, and extend its sphere of usefulness. This is evolution. It is a fact, a law and not a theory, and its possibilities are as boundless as the imagination. The work of ages begun by nature has no apex. Evolution is advolution. It does not stop with the organic; its future is greater than its past, and from spirit-people only can come such facts as will make the physical world comprehend its possibilities.

XVI. Beyond The Atom

WE are told that atoms, through their power to change from one form into another, always follow the law of definite proportions; and that, in obedience to that law, they are amenable to the will of intelligent force. Outside of the operation of this law, they are incapable of being controlled in any known way. This would place them beyond the category of mortal mind, and make them, to some extent, superior to it. The atom holds within itself the properties of all forms and material things. It is the central point from which universal creative energy proceeds. It is the basis of all power that manifests form or force. It is indestructible in its nature; its existence is regulated by definite and fixed laws; and the substance into which it enters is held in position, as regards form, by the inherent energy of the atoms composing that form.

The atom, alone, has eternal duration of form, for it alone has the power to enter and dominate all other forms. It has no master except force, and to force alone is it amenable. Whether force precedes it, or is co-existent with it, is not now known; but^ probably, the same force which impels the atom upon its course with unerring precision, precedes it in the province of creative evolution. Beyond the atom is an intelligence which has imbued it with these properties and powers.

Man, reflecting the image of wisdom, boastingly asserts his authority over the rest of creation; but he is ever subject to the power *vested in the atom,* and only as he reflects the activity of the elements in his own structure, is he able to rise to an intellectual status whereby he can comprehend the more simple laws of constructive energy.

This is one of the reasons why we are obliged to take into serious consideration the *existence of invisible intelligences,* who understand how to manipulate the forces distinctly pertaining to the evolution of the world of spirit. Numerous experiments have demonstrated beyond question that they exist. And that spirit-intelligences understand how to affect these forces in form, is neither untrue nor absurd. The failure to grasp this fact is really due to our own contracted minds, which are prone to limit all elements to the sphere of phenomenal physical conditions. We must conclude, then, that the same energy which controls and directs the movements of atoms and molecules, which sustains in position, and directs the course of stars and constellations, which finds life-expression in grass and in grains, in weeds and in flowers, in forest trees and in all vegetable growth, applies equally to man whose physical body, like all vegetable matter, is composed of atoms.

As we ascend in the scale of conscious intelligence, the universe opens to our mental vision and gives us a basis for a broader conception of the intelligent force underlying the physical universe. When we consider the law of life, in all its varied relation to visible and invisible form, we understand how rational is the proposition that the great law of nature has its existence entirely above and beyond the physical realm. Theologians of the past, having no definite knowledge of creative energy, formulated a theory of the source of life ending in mere abstraction. Their logical position was this: "God is the source of life. God made the world and all upon it and in it, by a fiat, a decree, of His own free will." This is only a confession of gross ignorance and manifests a childish inability to produce satisfactory evidence concerning the subject. It shows the utter incapacity of the human intellect, dominated by superstition, to discern any relation of force beyond the range of physical senses.

Human progress may be rapid or slow, according to the effort expended; but the atomic forces are ever at our disposal, and we can move forward as we will, regardless of the craft of men or the opposition of ignorance. It must be acknowledged that the human intellect is unable to discern the relations of cause and effect in many of the problems that come before it for solution; and there lingers around the subject of the *life action of the elements* an idea that they are as far beyond the scope of intelligent explanation, as the *results* themselves are beyond the unorganized forms of the same elements.

What, then, is this energy, this intellectual force, which is back of the atom and expressed in or through it? What or who controls and directs its movement with perfect precision? Some call it energy; some force; some nature; and others call it God.

The word "God" is so indefinite, I doubt if those who utter the word with reverence, have ever formed any definite idea of the creator; and those who think He has personality, have little comprehension of the universe. If God has personality, in the accepted sense of the word, He must be a person with extraordinary powers and intelligence, for, by the law of comparison, ideas themselves must be formed.

God, I am told, means simply Universal Good. Apart from the philosophical signification of the word, this is its true philosophical import. Let me explain what I understand by the divine principle. The life force in all things,— the intelligence that directs matter in movement and works out the laws governing all things,—is but the intelligence of all those who have lived in this sphere or inhabited other planets, who, having progressed beyond the physical plane, have mastered all knowledge and are working in perfect harmony, as one mind, in a sphere of perfectly harmonious development; and in that sphere the mind power is universal, permeates all space, and finds individual expression in all life forms. The inclination within us to do right and to shrink from wrong is that atom of Universal Mind which, clothed with matter, becomes a man, while the same law that governs an atom, governs all mankind. The energy of the atom is its potential life-force, and the life force in it or in us, is Universal Good working out its destiny.

Life-force dominates all matter. The whole physical world outside of planetary action and natural growth and change, may be largely governed, in its movement and direction, by man.

Matter operates on matter, and inert substances in the physical world move only when directed by the material mortal mind.

The power of even one man's thought is beyond present comprehension. Man has taken iron, and fashioned it into machinery with which he moves great buildings. He has taken coal, converted it into steam, which, confined and released, utilizes energy that will transport material to the limit of land; then, using like energy, he propels great ships over the sea, fashions sails and makes the very winds do his will. He has put a turbine under the waters, whose fail he directs; on the shaft a dynamo, which the waters whirl; he gathers and condenses the very ether into what we call electricity. Mind is all creative. The hands but fashion what the mind conceives.

Not content with dominion over matter sensible to physical touch, he reaches out into the atmosphere, and utilizes the very elements,—and the end is not yet. Only he who consciously progresses comprehends the possibilities of progress. Does the mastery of mind end with physical dissolution? Does death increase or diminish opportunity? Life would be futile if all the struggle for development were to end with earth-existence. While our conception of mind domination has its limitations, its possibilities are even now beyond our comprehension and one fails to appreciate the power of even a single mind. The energy produced in the electric current is as marvelous to the savage as the energy of the atom is to science, and as little understood.

We may follow, step by step, mind-power in mortal man, witnessing his control and his mastery over matter and the elements of the air; but, before we reach the limits of definite thought, we appreciate in a limited way that, if individuality and mind continue beyond the physical domain, man is still exercising his mental faculties, still studying and applying his intelligence to obtain greater control over matter in the conditions of the life beyond,—and the nucleus **of** all this action is the energy of the atom.

Whether we can appreciate this fact or not, it is true that, as men grow in knowledge in the after-life, they work in greater harmony with each other; many minds, in many ways, work as one, much more there than here, and accomplish greater results in a thorough, practical way. Science attributes these results to the unknowable; those of less understanding, to God. The individual mind when released from its physical environment acquires greater mastery and power. Considering what men can do here and their control of the electric force alone; knowing that they live on in a constant state of progression, it requires no stretch of imagination to perceive that the same persons are ever exercising their reason and obtaining greater knowledge, increased efficiency and usefulness, and, as this is being accomplished, their dominion over matter increases. Man creates nothing; the energy that he uses was dominant in the atom at the beginning; he, by combination or decomposition, only gets another and greater expression.

Beyond the atom we find minds, that have at some time lived in a physical body, working in unison and combining substances that will endow matter with energy which will give expression to life force in the material. In fact, all there is, is mind, matter is the substance used in its physical expression only; mind alone is creative energy. Men, who have lived in this or some other planet or constellation of the universe, who have passed out of the physical world that they inhabited, have, after countless ages of progression, reached the sphere of knowledge, and work as one, finding expression in every form of life and force. Thus, beyond the atom we find, not God, but mind.

I once asked a spirit: "What is the force that finds expression in the atom?" He replied:

"It is the individual man, purified and developed to his highest capacity, and blended with other minds in a similar condition. Guided by the knowledge gained through vast intervals of time, and working in perfect harmony with each other, these minds are the controlling power of the universe. I say 'controlling' for they, in turn, are but instruments of the dominating laws of the universe. They make these laws, to be sure, but, these laws must be of one kind for *nature aspires to good*. They progress through a condition of intellect bounded by mortality, into a new development until the circle is completed, and a harmonious whole is formed. It is a vast subject to comprehend, and yet, once grasped, it is perfectly clear. What other theory calculated to satisfy rational minds, has ever been put forward, than that the intelligence should ultimately become so effective that, combined with all the rest, it should be the highest force for good? Everyone must feel, and appreciate, that thus only can the inferior order of minds be guided toward their ultimate goal. This is the only philosophy of existence which, when once fully understood, seems true, reasonable and convincing."

XVII. The Subconscious Mind

THE physical and the spiritual universe are closely interrelated. There is a physical brain and there is a spiritual brain, and they have relations to each other which cannot be ignored. All that is physical has its duplicate in spirit, but all that is in spirit does not have its duplicate in the physical.

It must not be forgotten that the earth-sphere is a natural world; and that the spirit-world is also a natural world. The relation of the one to the other is, therefore, natural. In a physical sense, mind is memory, thought is that which feels, which wills,—the conscious subject. Again it is the ego, the soul, the spirit; it is all these and something more; *it is something that catches suggestion from the intelligence of other spheres and expresses it in this sphere.*

Let us now deal with the world of mind, with special reference to the subconscious mind, which immeasurably transcends in importance the physical domain. Science has tried hard to explain many things on the hypothesis of "mental telepathy," "secondary personality" and "subliminal consciousness" in its efforts to understand spirit-phenomena; when, as a matter of fact, it knows but little about the subject. Suppose one mortal should try to send a thought message to another at a distance. What natural law is used? No wire; no wireless instruments; merely a sentence sent out through space, encountering in its passage countless millions of other thoughts of different kinds. What is the motive power? What directs its course? And, if it should, by chance, reach the ear of the person intended, by what process will he hear something that comes in the silence, but not out of it? Why advance a theory that is not based on a single known law? The Marconi system has instruments perfectly adjusted and in tune with each other, and, by laws that are understood, are able to receive a signal sent by the sending to the receiving instrument. We, too, have an instrument, to wit—the human brain, far more complicated and wonderful, and the time may come when mental telepathy is practical, though it is not now.

I know that thoughts and messages are at times carried from one mortal to another, but it is a rare occurrence. Ordinarily some one in the spirit-world hears the message, and becoming a messenger, finds the person for whom the message is intended, and impresses the words on his subconscious mind. This will be easily understood when human beings come to appreciate this community of spirit-people who dwell about, yet not with, us. Mental telepathy is, in fact, suggestion, much used by spirit-people. In aiding and directing the conduct of mortals such practice is common with them, and it is hard for us to differentiate between self and spirit-suggestion, so vague is the border line. Thought-suggestion between mortals is possible, but unusual.

There is but one self, but one individual atom of good in any person; and though that person may, at times, do and say things of which he has no knowledge and which cannot be accounted for by any known physical laws, that fact does not double, or change his personality. This is called "secondary personality." It is possible for spirit-people, upon rare occasions, to take a mortal out of his body, and entering into his living body, use his vocal organs. This is not uncanny, but simple and natural. If one, under proper conditions, tells of things of which he had no previous information, which, upon investigation, are found true, it was not another self but someone else talking; for by what law could that second self know what the first self did not know? And so with "subliminal consciousness," that is, something below sensation: the doing of acts without being aware of it. These words, coined by men seeking a material solution of problems not understood, have no justification in fact, they are misleading and the theory is erroneous.

When those who coined the words "mental telepathy," tell us what law is used in its operation; when they tell us how it is possible to have two personalities; and where the one is and what it is doing when the second self is present; and a little of what is meant by "subliminal consciousness" they will be entitled to more consideration.

The answer to these last two propositions is the spirit-hypothesis based on fact and founded on natural law. The subconscious mind, when understood, will eradicate those senseless words from the vocabulary, and solve many problems with which man is struggling.

I asked one far advanced in spirit-life to tell me of the subconscious mind from his point of view, and he said:

"The conscious mind is one controlled by yourself. In it are held all the material parts of your thoughts,—I mean those connected with and controlled by, earth-things. The subconscious mind is the one controlled by psychic forces entirely. It is the spiritual brain of man. I mean, that it is subject to the laws of vibration, which the other part of the brain is not sensitive enough to catch. It is the subconscious mind that gets suggestion from spirit-people, the connecting link, or battery, that for an instant holds the suggestion, and passes it on, to grow into a thought or impulse. The subconscious mind does not retain suggestion. It is the embryo thought, which takes definite form only as it reaches the conscious mind."

From this concise statement of fact it is evident that all the strange phenomena, which science has been trying to solve and to which it has given many names, consist, ordinarily, of spirit-people hearing the spoken words or seeing the written message, then finding the person desired and impressing the words or message on the subconscious mind or spiritual brain. When the conscious mind catches the suggestion and makes it a part of the material thought, we have what is called mental telepathy, which, in fact, is, except on rare occasions, all accomplished by spirit-people acting upon the subconscious or psychic brain.

Speaking on this subject generally, one in the world beyond said:

"It is well, always, to consider that a result is equivalent to the effort put forth. The intensity and constancy of a thought are a positive force. A thought, bearing upon any particular subject, having been thoroughly established in the brain, grows just as a plant grows from the seed. As the development of that seed will be proportionate to the conditions of the soil and the amount of sunshine and moisture, so is it with the growth of thought."

"Thought is planted in the human brain by the next great power beyond mortal man, sown in the form of suggestion, and, as with the seed sown by the master hand of man, so it is with the suggestion sown, largely, by the master hand of spirit forces. Some are given birth and grow and fully develop in all their importance and beauty; but many —by far the great majority—fail of birth. Where the latter condition prevails, the human brain must, by a process of purification, be made receptive until it can catch and give birth to the seeds of suggestion sown.

"Progress is the grand object of nature. This word 'progress' is one of mighty import to the material world, *and true progress is possible only when those who have advanced to a higher plane help those who are still struggling upward. This applies to all things, material, intellectual, and spiritual. Nature has imposed on us spirit-beings the duty of assisting those mortals in the body by such suggestion as we can impart to them through the subconscious brain; and so, likewise, there are some among us to whom suggestions are imparted by those in the grade immediately above us.*

"As on earth there are weeds, as well as useful grain and beautiful flowers, so among your people are there apparently worthless mortals; but who can say when or how the weeds, following the great law of progress, will evolve into useful or beautiful plants; and yet, as simple weeds, may they not serve a great, if hidden, purpose? And so with those among you who, according to your judgment, appear worthless. Do not forget that the same Master-hand that created them, created you; and that it is better not to criticize, but to endeavor to get an expression of the intent of their condition. Always have charity. If you do not possess it, secure and cultivate it.

"What I have said this beautiful Sunday morning, is a sermon to you, the lesson of which is: Let those thoughts that come as suggestions flashed upon the sensitive plate of your brain, upon your subconscious mind, grow. Cultivate them. As they develop, they gain in strength, and as they become strong in themselves, they can, by their own strength, and because of the emanations they throw off, accomplish deeds. Whatever conies to the subconscious mind must be at once grasped and held, if you would make it your own. Then the thought is fashioned and developed to become again a part of the universal stream that flows into the Eternal Mind."

The average so-called man of science seems determined not to accept the spirit hypothesis of psychic phenomena, and offers many other explanations while going through his erroneous process of elimination; but truth existed before, and will be after, his futile struggle is over, and he may be among the last to understand this simple law.

Sir Oliver Lodge, the foremost scientist of the present day, who acknowledges the existence of an invisible world of spirit-people and has proved it to his own satisfaction, says: "The object is to get, not something dignified, but something evidential." It seems to me that when one has proved the existence of a thing, he would like to know something about the thing proved and not try to prove it again. Having long ago proved the existence of the invisible world of spirit-people, I have not sought for an accumulation of evidential facts, but rather for something dignified from the inhabitants of that world. Whether or not such facts have been given me these pages will answer.

XVIII. Spirit-Suggestion

HAVE spirit-people any influence on our daily thought and action? If so, to what extent and by what process?

To bring ourselves intelligently to the question, we must appreciate, as we have never done before, that those out of the physical body are people,—as they were before dissolution; that their bodies are composed of matter differing from ours only in vibration; that they live and inhabit what we know as space; move over and walk upon the city's busy streets; go into and out of homes, as freely as before; and are silent witnesses of our daily thought and action. They travel at will, along the old highways, stay about the homes they loved and built with infinite care and ceaseless toil; see us and know our daily wants, desires and ambitions; and are acquainted with the discords, as well as the harmonies, of our lives. By law many become co-workers in our struggle for development. I know the limitations of the human mind and its inability to grasp this simple proposition, more important than the accumulation of wealth, and wish for many tongues that I might speak in all nature's dialects and languages, and bring this simple fact home to all the men and women who inhabit this globe, for it would revolutionize the conduct of mankind and enrich the world.

There are some truths that cannot be told too often; there are truths that, no matter how often told, seem to make no impression; there are some soils which no matter how perfect the seed or how thickly sown, give little return; and so, in many ways, we tell over and over again what follows dissolution, finding now and then a fertile brain.

All knowledge is the result of suggestion, which may be divided into three classes— physical, mental and spiritual, (a) *Physical;* that which is objective. Everything we see or hear in nature makes its impression on our minds. Something is by that process suggested to our senses, and, to the extent that we grasp and understand, we make it our own and thereby the sum-total of our knowledge Is increased. One in spirit-life, who has given many lectures, said on this subject:

"Come with me through the walks of life, and see the manner of men we can help. It is not the arrogant fool who says in his heart: 'My way is the only way,' nor yet the man who weakly fears to trust his own instinct and vacillates falteringly between the opinions of man; but it is the sane, quiet thinker, who is willing to listen to all arguments and to choose wisely those that appeal alike to his heart and brain. Such we can assist by spirit-suggestion. Without his being conscious of it, we can often guide his thought along right lines, because he is fair minded.

"Suggestion is one of the strong factors in the life-force. As you said this morning, all things have their power of suggestion. Does not a low saloon throw out its vile suggestion to all men? Whether this emanation entices or repels, depends upon the man, but its surrounding influence is felt strongly, and the suggestion is evil. A beautiful rural scene is helpful with its suggestion of peace and harmonious coloring. And so it is through all phases of life. Hence all should seek the best, and, unconsciously all do aspire to it."

(b) *Mental;* that is, by deduction or reasoning from one known cause to its effect, something more is suggested. By this method we prove facts previously unknown. An illustration of deductive reasoning is found by accepting what is known as a fact that "nothing in nature can be destroyed." From this proved hypothesis, we find that our mind, or soul, is a part of nature just as much as the earth itself, and more important. The Master-mind that created all things has not planned the annihilation of its higher forms, and preserved the lower. That would be at least an injustice. Man has proved that it is impossible to destroy an atom. We prove by the process of deductive reasoning, which is really the highest form of demonstration, that a human soul cannot be annihilated; and, having reached that stage of mental development, it is only a step to prove, by laws as certain as those pertaining to the physical, that the spirit of man, as a fact, is not destroyed. This we know because, with many others understanding the elementary laws of vibration, *we have talked with them*. The inductive method will help to confirm the conclusions of the deductive on the subject, for if the spirit of man be indestructible, why should it be impossible for earth-dwellers to communicate with those who have left the earth? Franklin was able to demonstrate the two methods; inductively he showed that lightning and electricity are identical, and, deductively, that houses may be protected by lightning rods. If spirit be seen by induction to be identical with mind, deduction will enable us to conclude that spirits, still in the flesh, can have direct relations with spirits out of the flesh.

(c) *Spiritual;* with spirit-people, thought is such a positive force, and takes such definite form and shape, that it is visible. Their language is a thought language and is as well understood among them as words among us. They soon lose all desire for physical touch or expression, finding the purely mental so much more intense; and, as they move in and out among the people of earth and see when and where they can do good, they, by a purely mental process, often suggest to us what to do or what not to do. Thus the suggestion of those who have passed out of earth-life comes to us as a moral guide, whose true origin many ignore because so many have absolutely no knowledge of what happens after dissolution. This form of suggestion we call intuition, impulse, inspiration.

Spirit-suggestion comes through our subconscious mind. Mind, whether in or beyond the physical, is a positive force in nature, more in fact than action, which is the result of mind; and spirit-people, desiring to influence our conduct to some desired end, retard their mental vibrations, and, at the same time ours increase until our vibrations and theirs pulsate more or less in harmony; then it is possible for them to make their thought our thought, and when we, guided by their suggestion, do some good deed with their co-operation, we increase in some degree the sum of Universal Good. But, because those beyond the physical are not always spiritual, some being on the contrary, of a low order of mentality, often depraved, as when in the body, with low instincts and base appetites, they, if our thoughts and desires are of a similar character, can reach our subconscious mind, and suggest that which will satisfy their desires and the results are base actions produced by both factors. Man is not a mere automaton, but a personality, deriving his progression from suggestions of people both in and out of the body; and it is difficult, so subtle is spirit suggestion, to tell with any certainty whether the thought that preceded the act was our own conception or that of some spirit working through our brain to do good or to satisfy his own selfish desires. For this reason one should weigh well what he has an impulse or desire to do. Good always precedes evil. First impressions are better than those which follow, because they are more spiritual.

The whole process of thought is the result of suggestion, without which ideas could neither be formulated nor expressed.

Knowledge would be unknown and evolution impossible, were it not for suggestion. The influence of the spirit-world is far greater than any mortal can comprehend because we are unable, so faint is the line of demarcation, to tell the origin, or source, of any thought.

In formulating this philosophy, I am unable to say to what extent intelligences beyond the physical have influenced my mind. My brain may have been, so to speak, a conduit of thought, and my hand an instrument to give physical expression to natural laws not generally understood by man. I cannot tell; I have not been conscious of any suggestions; but, knowing, from my conversation with spirit-people, the subtle power of suggestion, I would not say that they have not had a very great influence in shaping this work. I have the greatest respect and love for many who have, voice to voice, proved their identity, and given me their knowledge. What they have taught I know; to just what extent they can influence our daily conduct and thought depends on their mental conditions and ours. It is, therefore, largely an unknown influence, but an important fact, which man should understand.

The life of spirits is intensely active and real; they have their work along those lines for which their experience in earth-life has best fitted them; they labor where there is the greatest need, where most good can be done. The ignorance of those in the physical world on this subject is very great and, as a result, their condition is so inferior to what it might be, that spirit-people, realizing the deplorable situation, spend much time in the earth-plane striving to enlighten mankind and to make them live better individual lives, a task which increases their labors and impedes their own progress.

I recall listening, not many years ago, to a boy not more than fourteen years old, playing the great masterpieces on a violin with marvelous technical skill. His intellect was not above the average, nor had he received any special artistic training, yet he could execute the most difficult music. One of our standard law-books, recognized as an authority, was written by a boy while at college. Fiske wrote philosophy in his teens. We have always had prodigies who were able, without much education, to accomplish great things; but there is nothing remarkable in this, after all; it means only that a master in spirit is able either to suggest and to work through their subconscious brains, or, in some instances, like the boy violinist and Blind Tom, to take actual possession of the body and brain, which, for the time being, is used as an instrument by a master-mind to give physical expression to his attainments.

What is true of the boy, is true likewise of the man. It is difficult, so great is the power of spirit-minds, so fine is the line of demarcation between self and their suggestion, to tell, at all times, what is self and what is suggestion. This mind of ours is like a stream having its source among the hills and flowing toward the sea. A thought to the right finds its way to the channel; another one comes from the left, and joins the current, adding volume and character; and when the stream reaches the sea of expression, it is hard to say how much of it came from the original source, how much is our own, or how much flowed in from surrounding conditions.

We hear a voice calling our name; we turn and listen; it suggests that some one would speak to us. We hesitate while the thought finds lodgement in the brain; and it, too, sets in action a line of conduct. That thought may have been generated by a process of reasoning, and, again, it may have been the suggestion of some spirit interested in our welfare. Spirits can call as well as those in the physical body; both can be heard, the first by the mind itself, and the last by the physical sense of hearing. And it is difficult for anyone to say, such is the feasibility and possibility of spirit-suggestion, whether one originates or obeys. Inspiration is spirit-aid and suggestion, nothing more.

XIX. The World's Desire

THIS is an age of greed. We, as a people, have drifted out upon the sea of selfishness, egotistic desire and devouring ambition, and set the many sails to woo the winds of fortune. This is an age of money. Every nation and every people have erected a throne on which wealth sits in state; they have placed upon its brow a crown of gold, and have decreed that the possession of money, with little regard to the manner of acquisition, should be the only qualification for this kingship of modern times.

Man, at the dawn of physical development, is shown this goal, and taught that money is power and the world's desire. He enters the strife and bends his energies, as others do, to grasp the greatest amount of wealth with the least possible effort, matching his cunning against labor,—mind against muscle,—artifice against simplicity,—and directs his thoughts towards wrenching from the hands of honest toil a portion of its legitimate earnings.

Does wealth ever ask what claim it has on the savings of labor? Why is it adding to its already vast store, while other hands are growing feeble from want, and shadows are falling on poverty stricken homes? Does capital ever contemplate the privation and suffering that must follow close upon the heels of cupidity and deception? Do captains of industry realize that, by directing their ability towards the concealment of base designs under the veil of enterprise, and by the misappropriation of the proceeds of honest toil, they are, according to a higher standard of ethics, guilty of larceny; and that by a law, as fixed as gravitation, the time will come when they, through laboring and suffering, in the life beyond the physical, must make compensation for every dollar acquired unjustly?

Consider what a future awaits those who make ambition their goal, and who succeed in seating themselves upon the throne of wealth by modern methods! It is a great misfortune to have false ideals, to worship at the shrine of money; but it is a far greater misfortune to succeed, and to hold unlawful gains, or more of nature's store than a simple life requires. That all should work and save against old age is proper; but that accumulations should greatly exceed the needs of existence, was not intended by the intelligence that planned all things. We see men in the morning of life preparing for the strife: so fast they rush, so eager is the struggle, so crowded the field, so elusive the object of pursuit, that each one thinks only of self. Like men in actual battle, they fight for mastery, never hesitating to push aside those in front or to trample on those under them; and what is the end for which they strive? Wealth? Yes, but not all, for with the advantages that money brings, come arrogance, pride, greed, and increased selfishness.

Of what real benefit to the world are the very rich? Some few do good by gifts that help the poor and needy; some endow hospitals where suffering is reduced; some give libraries; others build churches and cathedrals. But the great majority hoard their gains and count their money; the love that should encompass all mankind is given to wealth. The greater portion of their thought has been spent in accumulating their hoard, and consequently they love it. This is the old age they have been preparing for, and, like the miser in his tower, they sing and chuckle as they count their gains and the gold coins slip through their fingers. So intent are they on accumulation that they are deaf to the call of charity. Surrounded by luxury, they have not come into contact with suffering; so busy and self-centered are they, that they have not had time to give words of encouragement to others. Nothing but self has found lodgement in their minds as they have been preparing for the future. What future? "Old age," one answers; but I answer: The future lies beyond the world of men! Will this gathered wealth support you through the coming ages? If another life follows dissolution; if natural conditions prevail, in the great beyond, and one has necessities there as here, what wealth has been accumulated for support in the community after this? Money being a material substance, is not taken, nor indeed can it be, for we see its distribution here. What, then, has been accumulated for support and maintenance out in the after-life where money is not king? All the wealth one can take with him into the after-life, is that which he gave away in this.

The thought that the *rich man here* may be, and usually is, the *pauper in the afterlife,* is startling in its possibilities and dreadful to contemplate. A man who has made money his God and worshipped at the shrine of gold, having no other thought, ambition or desire, in earth-life, is poor indeed if his hoard cannot be taken with him, for poor he is in all else, in a world where kind and thoughtful acts and deeds are the standard of wealth.

When the fact can be driven deep into the human heart and brain that after the material life, out in the great hereafter, one lives a life similar to this, and that he has necessities, actual wants, and desires that money will not satisfy; appreciation of what true wealth is, and how to gather it for one's eternal good, may dawn upon the minds of men.

Contemplate the after-life, where money is not used! The occupation of most people will be gone, they will find themselves disqualified for any other position, ignorant and helpless in a world of activity; then will come appreciation of the lost Atlantis men call opportunity. Upon the pages of memory will be written: wasted energy, false ideals, worthless ambitions, erroneous conceptions, ignorance of the simple laws of nature,—and selfishness will find itself a pauper, in a world of plenty.

In the next life, I am told, the only way to gain advancement is by helping others; in this way only is knowledge gained, for by contributing their efforts to greater good the Master Intelligence has provided for the individual advancement of spirit-people. Each builds his own stairway to the heights of knowledge,—"all for one and one for all,"—that is the law of their progress when they have emancipated themselves from earth conditions. Material wealth is only for a day, as time is counted. What the good man does enriches him here, and becomes a part of his own self for all that we call eternity.

If "doing good" is the only wealth that one can carry away into the after-life, how shall it be with those who have thought only of money, grown indifferent, cold and hard, and have lived this life for self alone? A picture of the condition of those in that class, whom we have talked with in the life beyond, is too terrible to describe. In earth-life they draw about themselves a mantle of arrogance and pride, closely woven of selfish thoughts and greed. Such is the garment that covers these naked souls as they journey on. Upon many not one ray of light shines; there is only darkness and despair; nothing penetrates the gloom but the chill of death and dissolution. The selfish worshipper of wealth is not only a pauper in a world of wealth, but an outcast in a community of harmony. The good men do "lives after them," the earth career becomes a part of them, and they a part of it. Good radiates light; selfishness is darkness—the absence of light—and so condenses the thought emanations as to encompass and obstruct one's vision. And so, on going out into the next life, the selfish enter into the condition they have created, there to remain, until, through suffering, the wish shall come, from within, to make restitution for a life of greed. Then will come the desire, unknown during earthly existence, to become a worker to help others—just for the joy that comes of doing good—and to find in this way only that "peace which passeth all understanding."

The wealth that all in this physical world should seek has not the ring of gold; it is gathered by right living, by helping others to live right, and by doing something each day that will bring joy to hearts that are sad, encouragement to those who falter, good cheer to those who are depressed, bread to those who hunger and clothing to the naked. Do something each day to make some mortal happier, and with each act let love go hand in hand. Thus only can mortals be enriched here and hereafter, "beyond the dreams of avarice," for one good act, sent out with love as its companion, will reach beyond the confines of the stars, and touch eternity.

XX. Homes In The After Life

ONE in the after-life gave me a description of the spirit home of a great, splendid mother, builded by the labor of love and ceaseless charity,— in the physical as well as in the spirit plane in which she now resides,—one who worked long and earnestly to make women understand the truth so that they might live nearer to the best in nature. Here is the description as it was given me:

"Before me is the interior of a splendid home, the home made by a spirit, created and builded by the thoughts, acts and works of one who, thirty-two years ago, lived on the material plane. The room opening before me seems like pure white marble with lofty ceilings; around the four sides runs a broad balcony supported by columns gracefully turned; from a point beyond the center is a broad stairway curving outward; at its foot, on each side, are niches filled with beautiful statuary. Going up the stairs now, I find each step a different color, yet all blending into one; on all sides of this upper gallery are windows through which come soft rays of light. Opening off the sides are rooms; and, as I look, a door opens and a beautiful spirit comes out, taking on, as she enters, the old material condition that she may be recognized. She has reached maturity in years, and has a face of rare gentleness—the beauty of purity,—she smiles as we describe her and her home to you. With her is a daughter just reaching womanhood; one that never lived the earth-life but was prematurely born. These two, drawn by the invisible bond of affection, have builded this home and made it rich with love.

"Passing down the corridor now, the mother's arm about the daughter, they approach the other end of the building and descend a stairway similar to the first, and go out upon a broad terrace, along walks bordered with flowers, into the garden of happiness. Turning now and looking toward a valley, I see many trees heavy with foliage, and through them I behold the waters of a lake, rich as an emerald in color.

About the vaulted room which I have described are many others of like material, filled with all that this mother loves. Books that she uses in her work are seen; pictures, created by acts of tenderness, adorn the walls. Musical instruments unlike those of earth await spirit-touch. This is a home where girls, just budding into womanhood, are taught purity—this is a mother's home, and suggests to you the possibility of spiritual surroundings. It was not builded in a day, but is the result of labor in the earth and in spheres of progression, where the surroundings are in harmony with spiritual development: the home of a good woman, builded by helping others."

I said to one of my friends in the afterlife, at another time: "Tell me of the homes of spirit people," and, in reply, he said:

"That is a most difficult thing to do, because earth-people expect to find everything so different, while, in reality, the homes here are practically the same as in earth-life, except that there is in the advanced spheres no discord, no lack of harmony, nothing but light, beauty, music, laughter, blended with earnest, thoughtful study. I am describing the home of a spirit who has grown to know the life-principle. There are many poor, struggling souls wilfully, or ignorantly, looking down instead of upward into the great possibility of the future, who are living in squalid huts which their deeds and thoughts in earth-life have made for them. Very few have beautiful homes ready for them when they enter spirit-life, for most people live in such ignorance of natural laws that they find insufficient shelter awaiting them, but the wise ones start to build by perfecting their way of thinking and by undoing wrongs on earth, and also, by helping others. No actual physical touch is given these homes, but, as the soul grows in beauty of thought and deed, the home grows to perfection."

"Are these homes as real to you as ours are to us?" I asked. "They are the abiding places of spirits who gather into them the objects of beauty they love, and there harmonious spirits come and go, as in earth-life. They are as real to them as yours are to you. But we look at things differently; we think them and the thought is expressed in waves that are visible and real as long as we hold the thought."

This is no flight of imagination. Let me bring home the truth by an illustration. Yesterday I purchased a country-place, which must be modernized and adapted to our requirements. I have been thinking what changes are possible and what I should like. It was a mental effort to take into consideration the situation and work out a plan. It was all done in thought. I can, by a mental process, see the change approach ; the graded lawns, the enlarged veranda, the great fire-place and the towering chimneys. In thought-vibrations these changes have already been made. They exist in mind which is matter, and all that remains is to have the mental plans put upon paper and sent to the builder, who will give them physical expression, construct in gross matter what now exists in refined matter. These changes are now thought creations; they exist in fact; I can see them.

So it is in the after-life. The home and environment are made by thought, created in spirit-matter, which is mind, and its beauty and grandeur is only limited by the purity and progression of our earth life. Those in the other life have their limitations, as we have; they must have knowledge and development and comprehension just as we do. We differ in our creations only in the manner of expression. The one must be suitable to physical; the other to spirit-requirements; both are first mental processes; one is expressed in gross matter, while the other consists of spirit-matter and spirit expression.

The next life, in its inception, is the sum total of this life, and nothing more. And the structure fashioned by our acts and deeds here, is that which we must inhabit when we enter the spirit-world.

The idea that all space is peopled and that in the universe there are no waste places, is not only startling but it must appeal to our reason that the Master Mind, in creating, so planned that all space should be of use and occupied, for some purpose. The thought world does not need the land nor the waters, nor the physical atmosphere, to subsist; passing beyond material laws, who shall say they cannot live and move in the invisible sphere about us—and surround themselves with thought creations? They live beyond and outside the physical bodies, beyond our vision, yet with us. While their presence is felt by the many, it is *known* by the few. This is the great misfortune of this so-called civilized world.

XXI. True Charity

CHARITY, in its general acceptation, has been identified with alms-giving; but why should a. word so potent, so beautiful, be so degraded? Spirit-people, with their higher intelligence, have told me that charity means giving to those in need our best and purest thought; and they have pointed out that on the earth-plane it is rather a mechanical than a spiritual action to distribute material things amongst others. How many, when they help those in need, give their best thought as well as material aid? True, material assistance is often indispensable; but, nevertheless, it should be only a stepping-stone to something higher and nobler. A charitable thought, sent out and transmitted by waves of psychic ether, will reach many souls in despair, and, perhaps, lift them to higher conditions in the material as well as in the spirit spheres. There are persons in earth life who are too poor to give material aid, but who, out of the richness of their benevolent hearts, give that which is better, more precious, more Godlike: loving words and kindly deeds. Such as these are never too tired to offer sympathy to those in need; never too weary to speak a cheery word to struggling neighbors. Such persons radiate happiness around them, and are continually sending forth the purest and best of which a soul is capable, and, when they go out into the after-life, they find that bread cast upon the waters does return.

It is my custom to ask of spirit-people to give some expression of their views on subjects under consideration, and in reply to an inquiry about charity, one said:

"And the greatest of all is charity of thought, without which the utmost gifts of money become as pebbles in the mouths of the hungry. Think of all as you would have all think of you. A thought once born grows to its fulness, not only by the good done to the individual, but, by its strength and goodness, it circles around, and after encompassing many in its kind embrace, rebounds to enrich the originator. Cultivate the desire to think kindly of your fellowmen.

Since thought dominates all actions, those who have evil thoughts are in danger of becoming evil themselves, though they may be unconscious of the fact. The mind flings out a radiance which, to some extent, sheds light on every avenue of life; if that radiance should grow feeble and your life selfish, you will ever remain in the twilight, and your outlook will always be limited; but if kindness and true charity dominate your thoughts, the radiance will continue rich and bright till its emanations reach the boundaries of hope and your soul is illumined by the crowning sun of happiness."

"The best way to judge character is to watch the faces of children who turn toward men. A good man loves them and has patience with them, and they turn to him as naturally as a flower follows the warmth of the sun. A bad man realizes their helplessness, and brutally vents his malignity on their small, defenceless heads. Such a man is not to be trusted in any walk of life.

Right rears its head majestically
And scorns disgrace;
Wrong seeks to hide, and turns away
To shield its face.

"Again, be generous to those to whom nature has limited her gifts, for nature compensates, and the time will come when all shall be equal. The poorly equipped for earth-life, will more easily acquire the lessons to be learned in the next, for those of patience and humility are learned already. Those who think differently are to be enlightened, not censured or ridiculed, for all who understand this truth of life's progression are entrusted with the great responsibility of teaching all who can understand; and you must get as close as possible to the lives of others, that your words may have weight.

"Let your hearts be fallow ground; plant therein the seeds of love, charity and purity; nourish them daily with the clear water of tenderness, and you will have a wonderful garden filled with fragrance and white with blossoms, and your life will become a part of the great life principle."

A minister, well known when in earth-life, said one evening to a gentleman who worked with me and helped gather the information now given the public:

"The intense satisfaction that is the constant result of right doing, based on honest purpose, is, in itself, sufficient reward for action. Of all the trite sayings of the Bible, the one that reads, 'What shall it profit a man, if he shall gain the whole world, and yet lose his own soul?' is one with the greatest meaning.

"Wealth brings many opportunities for good and for evil; in fact, more for the latter than the former, as the besetting sin of mortal man is selfishness, and the possession of great richness allows of a free expression of that greatest of all causes of trouble. The true and full meaning of the word 'selfishness' is in every way opposite to the most beautiful word in your language 'charity.' Shorn of their meaning, as applied to money, they are the negative and positive of man's character. The fullest opportunity of giving expression to these two opposite words comes with the possession of great wealth. The understanding of the full meaning of these two words is the truest index of a man's character. The ability to make one's life the embodiment of that wonderful word 'charity/ and to understand that other word 'selfishness' so as to avoid it, is the true test of mortal man's ability to control himself.

"Self-control is man's perfect condition. To know charity and practice its meaning; to know selfishness and keep it from you: this is self-control. This state of existence is as near perfection as the earth-tied mortal can hope to get. You have been chosen, one among many on your side of life, to bring certain great truths to the people of the world. In advance of the time, you are to be prepared for the time of your usefulness, and this is one of the moments of laying before you certain truths. To teach the truth, the teacher must be truthful; to induce others to accept pure and honest principles, the teacher must be pure and honest himself; to set certain facts before others, the teacher must be above criticism.

"You may honestly atone for those things that have so far occurred in your life, by making amends to those to whom you are indebted. So far as the errors of your past life are concerned, you have well and strongly conquered their chief cause, and you need no longer fear them. You have henceforth no excuse to do otherwise than to follow the honorable and ennobling instincts of your nature. Guard well your actions, that they may not be open to criticism from others; and particularly from the one of all others from whom you cannot escape,— your own self. You have been, and you are being weighed in the balance; and so much is expected of you, that you must not be found wanting.

"Remember that wealth brings the opportunity to give expression to what is best in your nature, and that you will find the only reward for doing good is that intense feeling of satisfaction that can come only as the result of a good deed, unselfishly done. It is well that man should earn his daily bread. It is the intention of nature that every mortal should struggle, for by no other means can he progress in the scale of being. This being so, one so situated that he can live without a proper exertion on his part, is unfortunate. Never forget this principle: the waste of money is not charity, but foolishness. You will find many practical ways to do good and to do it in the right way. A clean tenant demands a clean habitation. A pure heart and a pure mind are the results of your own efforts so to keep them.

"Charity is not a formula; it is thought clothed with a kind act. Cultivate charity in judging others; try to draw out the latent good in them, rather than to discover the hidden evil. We must do this, if we would rise to the full glory of our privilege, to the dignity of true living, to the supreme charity of the world."

XXII. "To That Mortal Would I Speak."

THE gentleman who opened the discussion on the "Attitude of Science" was himself, while in earth-life, a great thinker, and has evidently made much progress as a chemist in the sphere where he now lives. He is fearless in speech, and has courage born of knowledge. It is a privilege that I prize greatly to discuss philosophy with him, and many of his discourses have found place in this work. After speaking on the subject above mentioned, I asked permission to use what he had said. With his consent, I give, in his answer, perhaps the most remarkable message that ever came from the spirit-world: "In so far as you are impressed with the thought that my simple words will enable you to give to the people of earth a clear and honest statement of the facts with reference to the change from one sphere to another sphere of usefulness, everything which is in perfect accord with, and which carries out the intent of that whole, which it so perfectly controls, you are welcome to use. If anything that I have said, or may say, can, in any degree, bring to the people of earth an appreciation of the future that awaits them, I am deeply grateful."

'One, older in spirit-life, and far—oh so very far beyond me, *bids me say:*'

"Upward and onward! Always lead the way, for climb ye must, whether ye would or nay! That omnipotent force that has fixed the destiny of all things, has so willed, and, struggle though ye do and will, to follow your self-impulse, and journey to and fro, yet shall your course lay onward and upward. In all that has been, in all there is, and in all you shall know as you journey on, that one intent is the manifest purpose. The *one supreme intent* ye of earth-life shall not and cannot know, and that is wise and just. But this ye may know, for your very peace and comfort: every change that shall overtake you, is but to prepare you for the next; and further knowledge is but a dream of your own fancy, that springs from the speculative intensity of your desire to know.

"Knowing all, would ye not be that All? And knowing all, yet not having the wisdom to make use of that knowledge, what blundering fools would ye be! Only as ye shall have wisdom to exercise just and proper care of such things as be, shall ye know the meaning of those things. The servant must ever be able to do intelligently the master's bidding, that he may be worthy of trust; and if he faileth, then must the master bid him begone, and another shall enter into his stewardship until he who hath failed shall be worthy, once more, of his master's trust; and, should he fail scores of times without number, yet shall he be set aside until he hath become his own master; and then only may he be a worthy servant to his master. And so I say unto you, *that* ye may learn concerning the future, that shall help you in the time that is; but beyond the simple knowledge of the fact that ye shall have answered unto you the great question of Job—asked by every son of woman from all time—*'Though I die, shall I yet live again?'* I answer unto you, saying to all in earth-life, Yea! You shall! Let that, then, suffice for I say once more to all men, through you, that no mortal can obtain knowledge of what lies beyond save through the sphere above that wherein he dwells, for all must pass from earth before reaching the spirit-sphere; those in the earth plane must receive all knowledge of the after life from those who have progressed into spirit-life.

"Upward and onward ye must go; and only by such a ladder, as ye shall have built, can ye mount. So it is well that ye build wisely and with care. Let the rungs be of good deeds, and ye shall mount quickly and joyously to great and splendid heights; but if ye are careless and slothful in the building, and heed not nature's laws,—and they are writ that all may read,—your advancement will be delayed by your failure, for each rotten rung must be replaced; and O ye of earth! If ye could but know the weariness of such undoing and redoing, more heed would ye give as ye rush onward through life.

"And so I say to you this: to know that ye live again, though ye die, is all ye need to know to fit you for the future; and if ye knew too much of that future state that ye shall enter into, it would unfit you for that state in which ye now live. Take ye no heed of the morrow, but see that ye so live, each day, that the morrow may find you prepared. True honesty, like charity, begins in one's own heart. It is far better to have committed an honest error and reaped no profit, than to have great profit and to have honesty gone from your own heart.

"This spirit gives me no name. He says it has been lost so long from his memory that he scarce heeded its going. As you respect a worthy man of much learning and honesty of heart, without regard to his name, so I reverence this other spirit; and I am indebted to you for the privilege of knowing him, as he came to me saying: 'To that mortal would I speak? "

XXIII. Truth At Last

THERE is not in the universe a single great problem that man can truthfully say he has mastered, and concerning which nothing remains to be found out. The laws that control this world and are before all energy and chemical action, are universal and in force in other spheres as well as this; they control all solar systems and worlds in space, therefore, a complete comprehension of those laws and their application requires more than mortal life. If this were not so, perfection would be practically immediate, and without process, and men would become gods here and now. The most brilliant men that have ever lived, knew but little of natural laws and of the origin and destiny of man; and until now have made but little effort to find them out.

The earth is yet so crude, our senses are so dull and our vision so limited, that we fail to realize those emanations and movements of refined matter about us, or the subtle and incessant play of forces around us. From a single ray of light shoot millions of electrons and corpuscles, the basic constituents of matter, smaller than the atom of hydrogen, striking blow upon blow, passing by and through us in their incessant warfare with the night, but we feel them not.

We do not realize the quivering and bending of the earth's crust under our feet, caused by changes of temperature and the pressure of atmospheric waves, nor do we hear the fermentations and oxidations of the soil in the changing seasons. We do not even yet know the exact nature of that ether which a recent investigator considers omnipresent and omnipotent. We see the action of gravitation, but know nothing of the medium through which it operates. We hear the wind soughing among the trees; but we do not hear the roar of sap up trunk and branch, the bursting of the buds as they bombard the air, or the speech of growing trees and flowers and grass among themselves; yet life, wherever found, has language.

The vibrations from out the abyss of space would reach our ears if they had more and higher octaves, or if our capacity for catching sound were immeasurably intensified ; we do not hear the clang of the planets as they ring down through their orbits, the explosive detonations of the sun, the wild dance and chant of the nebulae, the comets' note of warning, or the rush of wandering matter of which worlds are made, which must send out impulses and tremblings through the ether to this planet of ours. We are at all times in a great sea. of intensely active forces and potentialities governed by a law of which we have little conception.

About us, but invisible to most, a nation, or rather many nations, of spirit-people, "live and move and have their being," more industrious, more active, more intellectual, and more energetic, then we; but, such is their intense vibration, we do not ordinarily feel their touch, hear their voices, or see their forms; but conditions can be made, and have been made, so that, notwithstanding our limitations, we may have speech with them, and know at least something of how and where they live, and what they are doing.

There is so much in nature that we do not understand, is it any wonder that, having kept our eyes so close to the ground, we have not discovered this spirit world before? We have made conditions where it became possible for us to know a little of those other people, and, even though many have not had this evidence, that does not derogate from the truth of the discovery, which must forever stand as another fact added to the sum total of human knowledge. The possibility of communication between mortals and those in the world of spirits, has been proved beyond doubt; and it now remains for men of genius to adopt new rules of demonstration, and to bring into this new field of research, the same intelligent action that is applied to the lower sciences and to increase our knowledge of the spirit as they have of the material world.

Those who, through ignorance or prejudice, decry a new discovery, and so prevent fair consideration, are enemies of civilization. The time has come for man to be free and to think alone. Neither the teachings of the so-called dead, nor the conclusions of the living, can change the facts which I have proved, or nullify a single natural law. Truth has neither youth nor age; it is, and ever has been, a brother to reason; it does not need the assistance of fame or science; it has never been in the keeping of any particular class of men; it is the heritage of all who live.

I look into the future and see the creeds and dogmas that, for centuries, have enslaved the human race, dead and obsolete laws in life's great statute book. I see knowledge take the place of faith and superstition; I see the awful fear of death banished from every human heart and mankind at peace. I see a world of thinkers, honest and free, teaching the gospel of truth, the religion of nature, and philosophy of metaphysics,—the new science of matter.

Let this fact sink deep into every human heart: the individual thought must at all times be kept clean and pure for this wonderous and ever active mind of ours is from day to day throwing the shuttle through the web of life, incessantly weaving the fabric of the condition that will clothe the naked soul on the threshold of the after life, and those in the great beyond watch beside the loom.

THE END

www.ingramcontent.com/pod-product-compliance
Lightning Source LLC
LaVergne TN
LVHW092052060526
838201LV00047B/1361